HOME

Classic Essentials for Easy Living

TARA DENNIS

PHOTOGRAPHY BY MARTYN RUSHBY

JAMIE DURIE PUBLISHING

PUBLISHED BY Jamie Durie Publishing

JPD Media Pty Limited
ABN 83 098 894 761
35 Albany Street Crows Nest NSW 2065
PHONE : +61 2 9026 7444 FAX : +61 2 9026 7475

FOUNDER AND EDITORIAL DIRECTOR : Jamie Durie
GROUP CREATIVE DIRECTOR : Nadine Bush

PUBLISHER : Nicola Hartley
DESIGN CONCEPT AND ART DIRECTION : Amanda Emmerson
DESIGNER : Sonia McAllan
PUBLISHING SERVICES MANAGER : Belinda Smithyman
STYLING : Tara Dennis
PHOTOGRAPHY : Martyn Rushby
EDITOR : Janet Hutchinson
PROOFREADING : Catherine Page

SALES AND MARKETING CONSULTANT : Robert Sarsfield

PRINTED BY : Tien Wah Press, Singapore. First printed in 2005
DISTRIBUTED BY : HarperCollinsPublishers Australia

© 2005 DESIGN : Jamie Durie Publishing
© 2005 TEXT : Tara Dennis
© 2005 PHOTOGRAPHY : Martyn Rushby

National Library of Australia Cataloguing-in-Publication Data

Dennis, Tara, 1969–
Home : classic essentials for easy living.

Includes index.
ISBN 0 9757355 4 3

1. Interior decoration.   I. Title.

645

Visit Tara's website at www.taradennis.com

Contents

Introduction

Everything we buy or own needs to be managed in some way – from how we choose our household items to the way we accommodate and care for them in our homes. It's all too easy to accumulate and lose precious space to what we don't like or use nearly enough.

Now my house is no different from any other. It's busy, and while my family all have work and school commitments, it's also a place we like to spend time relaxing in.

For me it's an ongoing challenge to keep on top of day-to-day living while still creating a sense of calm and a place where we all feel at ease enough for it to be home, and yet there's enough order for it to work. And by work I mean having belongings and spaces that are comfortable and good looking, as well easy to keep tidy and clean.

A home needs to be equipped in order for it to perform the way you need it to, so you don't become a slave to it.

Solving decorating and design problems is all about finding what works for you and what doesn't. It's about adapting and refining what you already have, and supplementing with what you don't.

It's really not about what fashions and brands are in – it's whether you and your family are happy and what you surround yourself with is both useful and performs well.

In my opinion, a home can never be complete without a framework upon which your style can rest. And by far my biggest decorating tip is to start with the essentials and build from there.

Tara

INSPIRATION

INSPIRATION

I adore creating and for as long as I can remember I have made things. Cooking, painting, sewing and decorating are just a few of my favourite pleasures in life and I suppose the real benefit of my hobbies is that now I design for a living, I can inspire others too.

But where does inspiration come from? Well, personally speaking, I think it comes from all around you. And since your environment can have an enormous impact on your spirit and sense of well-being, I believe that, where possible, if you can improve and enjoy your surroundings, you will ultimately feel happier as a result.

A wise soul once told me that many people open their eyes but seldom see. So wherever I go, and whatever I do, I try to remain completely aware and conscious of my surroundings. I also try not to tolerate clutter if it leads me to feel stressed. And I take the time to make a few simple changes, which can often make a huge difference to the quality of my everyday life.

Inspiration can come from what you love to do the most and how you like to relax. Realising this can be a useful clue for unlocking some of your best ideas and from this you can feel energised and learn to start creating.

I find travel enormously inspiring and believe it really does broaden the mind as well as awaken the spirit. For me there is nothing quite like being in foreign lands to revitalise and energise the soul. New territories inspire me; they heighten my awareness of colours, sounds and smells. Where possible, I document what I see and the new ideas I may have as a result of my journey by writing, sketching and photographing along the way.

But even when time or money doesn't allow me to wander far, I still enjoy the creative stimulation of exploring books, magazines, television and the internet. When I'm feeling tired, I find these mediums are invaluable for inspiring me to consider fresh ideas and new techniques.

To decorate a room or even a whole house, the most important part of the process – and the one which makes it work – is to start when feeling inspired, then build around an idea and keep focused with a consistent design plan.

So look for your own inspiration and set about making a difference to your world. Once you start, you will find it's really not all that difficult.

Your spirits really can be lifted just by having a good sort-out of your belongings or by adding a splash of colour to a room. Paint up some old furniture or add some natural accessories and I guarantee you will feel a whole lot better for your efforts.

STYLE

Creating a functional as well as stylish home is simply a matter of choosing the basics wisely and finding better ways of storing and displaying your belongings. Then, you add your own individual style by grouping together things you love and need, whether old or new.

My philosophy for decorating is to furnish your home with honest, classic and simple materials. For all of the basic household items I buy the best I can afford and search for timeless, elegant styling and comfort.

I choose basic colours and furnishings in a variety of textures, which can easily be mixed and matched. The true beauty of classic styling is its ability to be added to and accessorised as often as you like using art, personal collections, cushions or flowers. Accessories are like the salt in the recipe – they add the flavour.

Attention to detail and handcrafting is also important. It adds character and warmth, as well as supplementing the more regimented look of mass-produced furnishings.

Things should not only look good, they also need to be easy to care for and maintain. Most of all a home needs to reflect the way you live and feel as though it has evolved, not just been 'done'.

STORYBOARDS

Before committing to any decorating or design project, I always take time to create a simple storyboard. This is something anyone can do and is a great way to compile ideas, pictures, samples and swatches and view them together as a group.

1. Start with pictures and ideas – which can come from magazines, catalogues and brochures.
2. Ask suppliers for swatches and samples.
3. Use white cardboard as a base. This will help to represent your colours accurately.
4. Arrange your swatches and samples to see how they all work together.
5. Like pieces in a jigsaw puzzle, play around until everything seems to fit and work together in harmony. Anything you're unsure of should be removed and replaced with something more suitable.
6. Once you're completely happy, glue everything down. Then use this storyboard as the basic style guide for your new design scheme.

PATTERN AND TEXTURE

I am passionate about how a room feels, possibly m<u>o</u>re than how it looks. And I am adamant it should invite you in with its subtle variations in colour as well as form.

Textural interest can add so much spark to a room. But it's worth keeping in mind that this doesn't always have to involve using a rash of bold colours or strong patterns.

A simple group of key colours and materials is the smartest way to decorate a home. Individual style can be added to each room using well-chosen accessories.

TIP : Tester pots are ideal for making sure you are happy with the colour you have chosen before committing to buying it. Paint out the entire pot on a large piece of cardboard, then prop it up against a wall and live with it for a couple of days before finally making up your mind.

Choosing a basic design palette is not just about paint. All of the surfaces and furnishings in your home combine to make up the overall feeling and atmosphere.

Where you can, try to add a wide range of complementing as well as contrasting textures to your furnishings. This can help to create an inviting space with plenty of visual as well as tactile interest.

Flooring can have an enormous bearing on how a room feels as it covers such a large area – and different types of wood, tiles, and stone all have individual colourings as well as textures and patterns. Rugs, carpet and natural floor coverings all have more obvious patterns and textures which can be used either individually or combined with other flooring types.

Fabrics and accessories in simple colours don't have to be plain and boring. Pattern, shape, texture and detailing can add the extra dimension needed to take something from looking very average to very smart.

TIP : Check swatch and paint colours in natural daylight. They will often look completely different to how they appeared in the store under artificial lighting.

PATTERN AND TEXTURE TIPS

- The beauty of solid colours and shapes is simplicity. The patterns, textures and detailing will all assist in adding flavour and interest to your scheme.
- Pattern should be used sparingly and coordinated using a common colour. Vary the scale for extra interest.
- Group objects for maximum impact and use colour, shape or texture to form eye-pleasing compositions.
- Plain, simply styled furnishings can be a canvas or backdrop against which you can create all kinds of looks.
- Avoid style overload and keep things simple. In my opinion, less is definitely more.
- Scale it up. Small artworks, furniture and accessories can make a small room seem smaller so go for fewer, bigger things for bold impact.

COLOUR

There are so many ways to make a room look beautiful and one of the most important is colour. Most of us know which colours we like and feel comfortable with but become confused when faced with endless choices of paints, fabrics and furnishings.

Colour itself is not confusing. But what can be is wading through hundreds of colour chips and swatches in order to arrive at a pleasing combination. I agree it's difficult, and I choose colour for a living!

While there is no such thing as right or wrong colours, a lot of the decision making boils down to personal choice. Of course some combinations do work better than others, but the best colour advice I can give you is to figure out what colours and styles you love, then work on gradually applying them to your home as time and money allow.

I would never advocate going shopping for new paint, fabrics or furniture without at least having a rough plan in your mind before you leave your front door. Do yourself up an ideas list of possible colours and textures – because it's a jungle out there and you will definitely need a strategy!

> **TIP** : *Look in your wardrobe! The colours you most often wear are a useful guide when selecting paint, accessories and home furnishings.*

HOW TO CHOOSE COLOUR

When most people think of colour, they automatically think of paint, but colour applies to everything in and around the home. So you need to think about which colours you like generally, then consider how you should apply them, whether it's in the hard or soft furnishings, paint or even the plants you choose.

Once you have established a basic group of colours you like, divide them into groups of main or 'body' colours and accents.

- *Body colours* should become your main backdrop and will be the major part of your scheme.
- *Accent colours* can be used to punctuate the main body colours for excitement and interest.

Body colours need to be chosen carefully for items which are reasonably permanent and cannot be changed on a regular basis. These include tiles, carpet, sofa and curtain fabrics, bricks, pavers, roofing and fencing. For all of these things, without exception, I prefer to select neutral, natural tones and textures and update with things I can change easily. In the house, this can be paint, accessories, towels and linens. Outside, the trims, timber and doors can be painted, and pots added, along with plants and trees with different coloured foliage.

COLOUR TIPS

- A new paint colour or a few simple accessories can revitalise and update a room for very little effort and cost.
- Colour can be used to enhance things you like, perhaps a painting or favourite collection.
- Colour can hide structural flaws or enhance a room's character and architectural details.
- If your room is an odd shape or lacks a particular feature or focal point, consider defining an area with colour.
- Make up a storyboard to help refine your colour and material selection.

NEW COLOUR SCHEMES

For new furnishings, fabrics and paint colours, think about how and when you use the room and most importantly how you want it to feel. It's also important to consider each room in relation to the others in your home, especially if you have an open plan layout. Generally you should select colours and materials in a sequence because rooms are often seen from one to another.

When redecorating, start by having a good look at the room with fresh eyes. Look at the walls, windows, doors and trims as well as the ceiling, floor and furniture. The general feeling and atmosphere of the room is usually established by these main areas as well as the quality and amount of light the room receives.

Make a 'wish list' of what you would like to change but do be realistic about your budget, skills and timing. It's all very well to say you can change everything all at once, but the reality for most of us is having to work around what is already there and can't be replaced that easily – things like windows, carpet and tiles, as well as curtains and existing furniture.

You may not especially like certain things, but if you can't afford to replace all you need to, you are better off working your design around what you already have rather than ignoring things because you don't like them. You may be surprised just how much better they can look when you include and work them into a fresh, new scheme.

The most important thing however is to try to keep things simple and consider limiting your colour palette for all furnishings throughout the house. This will not only unify and create a sense of calm but will allow you to update the look each season simply by using accessories.

COLOUR AND LIGHT

The colours of a room never remain constant and can change throughout the day according to different lighting and weather conditions. Because of this, colours should be sampled in as large an area as possible and observed over the course of a few days before making a final decision.

BY DAY

- A room which receives plenty of natural light allows a wide choice of colours and can be decorated with the palest of shades through to intense bolds and brights.
- Without good lighting, naturally dark rooms which receive little daylight will never come to life and will always appear dull. A combination of overhead, spot and lamp lighting will brighten the space.
- Dark rooms will look stunning painted with richer, deep shades and lit artificially, even by day.

BY NIGHT

- Artificial lighting will make colours appear very different to what they are during the day and can also vary according to the type and number of lights you have.
- Overhead lighting can be harsh and appear to drown out colour. It can also create dark shadows in areas where the lighting is uneven. This can be softened and controlled by using more lights as well as dimmer switches.
- Lamp light can be very flattering for colour at night and should be considered in addition to overhead lighting.

Natural

Natural and bleached colours form the very backbone of my design principles and I base all of my ideas around natural fibres, textures and materials. Apart from being immensely classic and comforting, naturals offer a solid design base which can be accessorised with practically any colour and style.

Naturals are the essential colours and textures of design, the perfect palette which will never go out of fashion.

ESSENTIAL NATURALS :
- Driftwood
- Charcoal
- Slate
- Raw Linen
- Coffee
- Clay
- Sea Sponge
- Taupe
- Storm Blue
- Cloud Grey
- Pewter
- Ivory

FOR CONTRAST, ACCENT NATURALS WITH :
- White
- Black
- Red
- Blue
- Yellow

ACCESSORISE NATURALS WITH :
- Pebbles, sand and shells
- Baskets, twigs and twine
- Silver, gold and pearl
- Foliage and succulents
- Pewter
- Silver
- White ceramic

DECORATE NATURALS WITH :
- Bleached and dark wood
- Clear and sea green glass
- Natural stone and tile
- Unbleached linen, pure cotton and hemp
- Black iron and wooden curtain poles
- Wool, sisal and jute floor rugs

For colour information please refer to page 194.

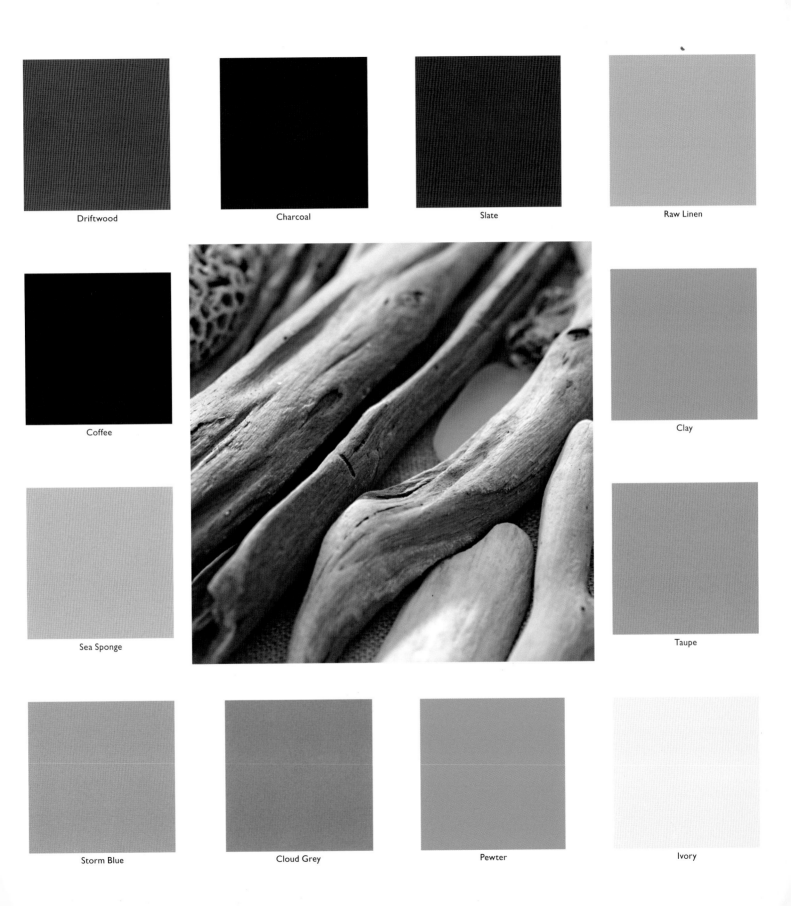

Driftwood

Charcoal

Slate

Raw Linen

Coffee

Clay

Sea Sponge

Taupe

Storm Blue

Cloud Grey

Pewter

Ivory

White

Perhaps the most understated tool of the decorator and yet the most common link, what makes white so effective is its subtlety. Far from boring, a room decorated completely with white may need nothing more, provided it creates interest and warmth with shading and texture. More commonly however, white is used to punctuate stronger colours and add relief where the eye needs rest.

ESSENTIAL WHITES :
- Cream
- Pure White
- Chalk
- Bone
- Nude
- White Smoke
- Pastel Pink
- Pale Mint
- Sherbet
- Shell
- Ice Blue
- Pale Mist

FOR CONTRAST, ACCENT WHITES WITH :
- Black
- Red
- Blue
- Yellow
- Green
- Violet
- Orange
- Pink
- Brown

DECORATE WHITES WITH :
- Ivory accents
- Dark as well as painted wood
- Bleached driftwood
- Pastel colours
- Toned colours
- Denim, navy and midnight blue
- Natural clay colours
- Stone and tile floors
- Clear and sea green glass
- Coloured or vinyl flooring
- Polished concrete, stone, slate and tile

ACCESSORISE WHITES WITH :
- Silver, gold and pearl finishes
- Wool, sisal and jute floor rugs
- Unbleached linen, pure cotton and hemp
- Black iron and wooden curtain poles
- Baskets, twigs and twine
- Foliage and succulents
- Glass
- White ceramic
- Pebbles
- Coral

For colour information please refer to page 194.

Cream

Pure White

Chalk

Bone

Nude

White Smoke

Pastel Pink

Pale Mint

Sherbet

Shell

Ice Blue

Pale Mist

Red

Pure forms of red like Chinese and scarlet are very powerful and need careful consideration and confidence when used as a main body colour. If you do like red but can't imagine using it across large areas, then consider it as an accent colour for fabrics, furniture and accessories. Little touches can add vibrant spark and excitement to an otherwise plain colour scheme.

ESSENTIAL REDS :
- Indian Red
- Leather Boots
- Ladybird
- Barn Door
- French Red
- Chinese Red
- Lobster
- Scarlet
- Fifties Pink
- Dolly
- Rosy Red
- Shocking Pink

FOR CONTRAST, ACCENT REDS WITH :
- White
- Black
- Blue
- Yellow
- Green

DECORATE REDS WITH :
- Polished stone, slate or tile
- The colours ash, black or charcoal
- Warm, textured fabrics like wool and felt
- Unbleached linen and pure cotton
- Denim blue for a fun and casual look
- Pink, both hot and pastel, for a vibrant effect
- Dark or light wood, but avoid mid tones of timber
- Bleached driftwood
- Olive green
- Pure through to soft whites

ACCESSORISE REDS WITH :
- Natural woven baskets
- Silver and chrome fittings and fixtures
- Blue and turquoise coloured accents
- Bowls and jars of black, grey and white pebbles

For colour information please refer to page 194.

Indian Red

Leather Boots

Ladybird

Barn Door

French Red

Chinese Red

Lobster

Scarlet

Fifties Pink

Dolly

Rosy Red

Shocking Pink

Orange

Orange includes shades ranging from the softest peach colour on a sea shell through to vivid pumpkin, spice, red coral and terracotta. In its pure form orange can be a little daunting as a main body colour but it does work well in the more yellow through to burnt shades. As an accent colour, orange can have as much impact as red while being perhaps a little sunnier and less formal.

ESSENTIAL ORANGES :
- Earth
- Terracotta
- Zest
- Red Coral
- Pumpkin
- Ruby Citrus
- Spice
- Turmeric
- Tom Yum
- Flesh
- Just Peachy
- Shell Pink

FOR CONTRAST, ACCENT ORANGES WITH :
- White
- Black
- Blue
- Yellow
- Green
- Red

DECORATE ORANGES WITH :
- Hot pink
- Grey blues to cool and soothe
- Slate grey flooring for a smart look
- Plummy burgundy to add richness
- Unbleached linen or pure cotton
- Painted, bleached or dark wood

ACCESSORISE ORANGES WITH :
- Dark banana leaf baskets
- Foliage and succulents
- Pewter and silver items
- Glass fittings and fixtures
- Clean, white ceramics
- Pebbles on plates or in jars
- Silver and gold picture frames or lamp bases

For colour information please refer to page 194.

Earth

Terracotta

Zest

Red Coral

Pumpkin

Ruby Citrus

Spice

Turmeric

Tom Yum

Flesh

Just Peachy

Shell Pink

Yellow

Yellow is a happy, easy colour to live with and works well in so many rooms. Soft, pastel yellows can be restful for bedrooms, bathrooms and nurseries while more intense ochres and olives work well in kitchens and family rooms.

ESSENTIAL YELLOWS :
- Olive
- Gold Card
- Provence Yellow
- Coin Gold
- Bees Wax
- Saffron
- Curry
- Smoothie
- Yellow Ochre
- Lemon Butter
- Vanilla
- Crackers

FOR CONTRAST, ACCENT YELLOWS WITH :
- White
- Black
- Blue
- Violet
- Green
- Orange
- Brown
- Red

DECORATE YELLOWS WITH :
- Ochre shades and white
- Buttery shades
- Soft blues and greens for a gentle contrast
- Magenta, which works very well with yellow ochre
- Slate blue for a beautiful accent
- Recycled red brick or terracotta floors
- Dark or white painted timber, but avoid pairing with pine and blonde woods
- Sisal and jute flooring to complement and add texture

ACCESSORISE YELLOWS WITH :
- Gold to add shimmer
- White-painted baskets
- Pewter and silver accents
- Pure white ceramics
- Jars of shells and pebbles
- Natural fibred baskets and rugs

For colour information please refer to page 194.

Olive

Gold Card

Provence Yellow

Coin Gold

Bees Wax

Saffron

Curry

Smoothie

Yellow Ochre

Lemon Butter

Vanilla

Crackers

Green

Nature offers the best selection of greens, so for inspiration I often go no further than the garden. Leaves, grass and new shoots all offer the perfect shading and colour combinations and can even be colour matched directly using today's computer software. For exterior house colours, I think it's essential to factor the foliage colours and types of your plants into your colour scheme. Such a simple thing can help your home complement and harmonise with its environment.

ESSENTIAL GREENS :
- Fig
- Racing Green
- Spearmint
- Deep Olive
- Bean Shoot
- Box Green
- Bronze
- Gold Leaf
- Vellum
- Gilded Lily
- Bleached Green
- Scandinavian Green

FOR CONTRAST, ACCENT GREENS WITH :
- Red
- Blue
- Yellow
- Orange
- Violet
- Black
- White
- Brown

DECORATE GREENS WITH :
- Hot pink for added impact
- Grey-blues to subdue
- Clear and sea green glass
- Slate flooring, complemented by blue-greens
- Unbleached linen and pure cotton
- Dark wood for added richness
- Bleached or painted wood
- Taupe for a classic feel
- Natural stone and tile
- Wool, sisal and jute

ACCESSORISE GREENS WITH :
- Baskets, twigs and twine
- Foliage and succulents
- Pewter and silver accents
- Glass fixtures and fittings
- Pure white ceramics
- Natural linen fabric
- Shallow bowls of dried seed pods

For colour information please refer to page 194.

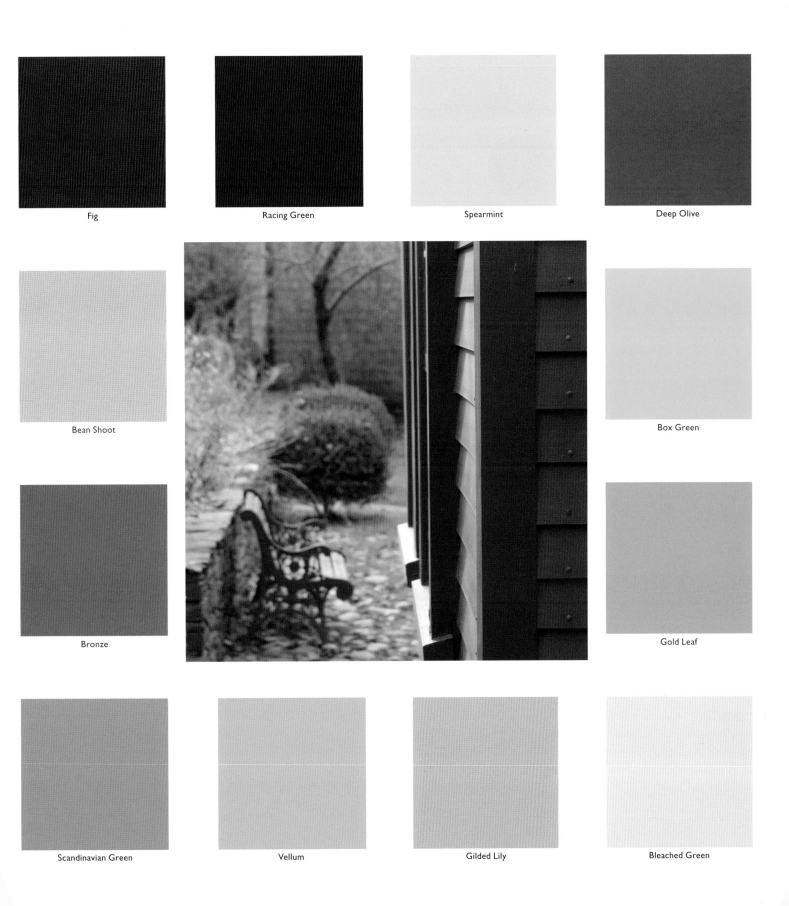

Fig

Racing Green

Spearmint

Deep Olive

Bean Shoot

Box Green

Bronze

Gold Leaf

Scandinavian Green

Vellum

Gilded Lily

Bleached Green

Blue

I use the sky as my palette reference for blue. The colour of the sky can vary so much over the course of a day. Early morning it can be soft and delicate with a just hint of yellow turning it pastel aquamarine. Storm clouds show grey-blue at its best, while the intense midday and early afternoon sun change the sky from a vibrant, warm blue to a violet blue later in the afternoon. Dusk brings a more vivid violet blue while evening deepens the blue to a royal then navy blue/black. So many natural and beautiful blues.

ESSENTIAL BLUES :	FOR CONTRAST, ACCENT BLUES WITH :	DECORATE BLUES WITH :	ACCESSORISE BLUES WITH :
• Blue Black	• White	• Light through to dark chocolate browns	• Pewter and silver accents
• Royal Blue	• Black	• Fresh shades of yellow and blue-greens	• Glass fixtures and fittings
• Bluestone	• Brown	• Coral, shell and terracotta	• Dark timber accessories
• Navy Blue	• Orange	• Bluestone or slate	• Plates of shells and pebbles
• Teal Blue	• Green	• Sisal and jute flooring for subtle contrast	• Lime green foliage in vases
• Denim	• Red	• Dark polished boards, which work well with violet blues	• Brilliant orange flowers
• Boat Blue	• Violet		
• Turquoise		• White-painted floor boards	
• Watery Blue		• Ivory carpet	
• Pastel Blue			
• Chalk Blue			
• Sea Spray			

For colour information please refer to page 194.

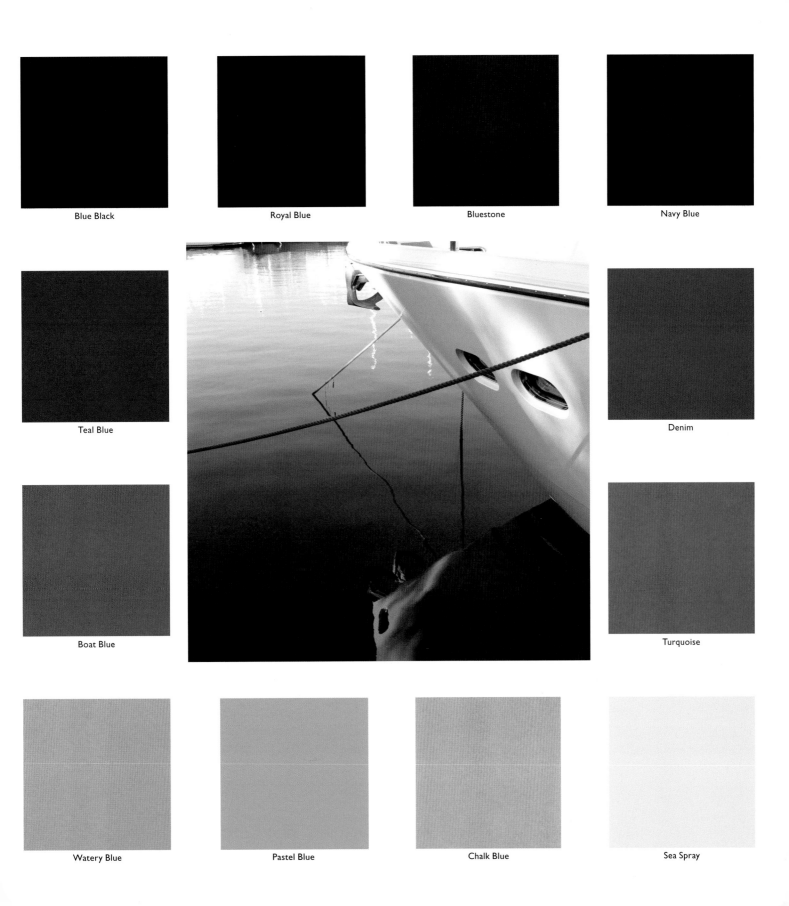

Blue Black

Royal Blue

Bluestone

Navy Blue

Teal Blue

Denim

Boat Blue

Turquoise

Watery Blue

Pastel Blue

Chalk Blue

Sea Spray

Violet

Violet is such a versatile colour in decorating. It can range from being sweet for a young girl's room to sophisticated when used in muted tones for walls and fabrics. I prefer soft, shadowy violets like taupe, lilac-greys and lavender as they are generally easy to coordinate and live with. These shades work especially well with crisp white woodwork and dark timber furniture. For something a little richer and more exotic consider blueberry, aubergine or plum.

ESSENTIAL VIOLETS :
- Royal Fig
- Aubergine
- Plum
- Raspberry
- Blueberry
- Roy's Iris
- Lavender
- Lavender Blue
- Cornflower
- Lilac
- Lilac Grey
- Lilac Blue

FOR CONTRAST, ACCENT VIOLETS WITH :
- Red
- Blue
- Yellow
- Orange
- Green
- Black
- White
- Brown

DECORATE VIOLETS WITH :
- Crisp white woodwork
- Fabric in dark chocolate browns or white
- Accessories in fresh apple or blue/greens
- Shell pinks and brick reds
- Grey slate flooring
- Sisal and jute flooring
- Dark polished and pine floors
- White-painted floorboards and furniture
- Plush ivory carpet, especially for bedrooms

ACCESSORISE VIOLETS WITH :
- Avocado green accents
- Pewter, silver and chrome
- Glass fixtures and fittings
- Pure white ceramics
- Jars of feathers
- Dark timber-grain furniture
- Bleached driftwood
- Pure white cotton and unbleached linen
- Fresh lavender
- Mirrors

For colour information please refer to page 194.

Royal Fig

Aubergine

Plum

Raspberry

Blueberry

Roy's Iris

Lavender

Lavender Blue

Cornflower

Lilac

Lilac Grey

Lilac Blue

INSIDE LIVING

cook

Cooking can be an absolute pleasure and made all the more enjoyable when your kitchen is equipped with quality tools which are well organised and easily accessible.

Benches need to be clear and cupboards sorted with room to spare. It has to be said however, that the more space we have, the more we tend to accumulate. So perhaps the answer is not a huge, new, 'dream' kitchen, but how you equip the one you already have!

— 60ml **1/4 cup** 2floz —

Pots'n'pans

I would bet that you have a jumble of pots and pans cluttering up your cupboards with odd shapes and sizes you rarely use! My suggestion is to have a good sort out and supplement old with new where necessary. Check if any pots are damaged or if lids are missing and think about how well each pan cooks your food. Are they easy to use and, most importantly, are they versatile? Selecting new cookware should relate directly to what you and your family like to eat — not what's on sale or how good a pot looks. We all have different tastes so how and what you like to cook should ultimately govern your purchasing decisions.

CHOOSING COOKWARE

Never underestimate the value of a good pan. After all, isn't great food worth going to lengths for? There is no point having the best recipe or buying all of the essential ingredients if you have pans that simply aren't up to the job.

Respectfully handled, a good saucepan will serve you well and is definitely worth paying a little extra for. I find it's best to avoid buying pans in sets – instead choose them individually in sizes and materials to suit your cooking needs. Look for versatility with styles that have several uses and buy the best quality, heavy-based pans you can afford.

Always look for long-term durability and consider ease of handling, storing and cleaning. Pans should have secure lids and handles which stay cool and are oven proof. Remember to check whether the pan is compatible for your cook top, particularly if it's an induction type. If you are unsure when buying new cookware, always read the information on the label or packaging about intended usage.

TIP : To reduce cupboard clutter, store your bulkiest pans away from the kitchen, either in the laundry or garage.

CHECKLIST

ESSENTIALS
- Saucepans
- Fry pans
- Stock or pasta pot
- Enamelled cast iron pot
- Metal colander
- Deep roasting tray with rack
- Shallow roasting trays

GOOD TO HAVE
- Clay pot
- Iron char grill pan
- Spatter cover

STAINLESS STEEL POTS AND PANS

Stainless steel cookware is a real personal favourite. It's relatively light, well priced and incredibly durable.

They say the best quality is grade 18/10, which refers to the chromium and nickel content in the alloy. A good quality stainless steel pan will generally have an 18/10 grade inner and an 18/0 grade outer base.

Stainless steel doesn't conduct heat very well so all of the best pans have a thick layer of copper or aluminium incorporated into the base and sides. This core spreads the heat more evenly across the bottom and up the sides of the pan, important in preventing those 'hot spots' which cook – and sometimes burn the food faster in some areas than others.

> **TIP** : *Cast or tubular stainless steel handles stay relatively cool and are more durable than other types.*

My favourite stainless steel pans :

- 16cm and 20cm stainless steel with a copper core in base and sides
- 26cm lidded fry pan with a copper core in base and sides
- 30cm x 36cm deep roasting pan
- 7.5–10L stock pot with lid

ALUMINIUM PANS

While traditional aluminium pans are lightweight and fantastic for conducting the heat, they do have one big disadvantage and that is their tendency to warp and react with certain foods. Because of this you will most often see aluminium used in combination with stainless steel or hard anodised for durability.

ALUMINIUM HARD-ANODISED PANS

Hard-anodised aluminium pans are not cheap but well worth the money for their performance and durability. While still being light in weight and great at conducting heat, the hard-anodising process makes the aluminium much stronger, preventing warping and food reactions which would normally occur.

My favourite hard-anodised non-stick pans :

- 16cm milk pan
- 20cm saucepan for porridge and sticky sauces
- 26cm saute pan with lid for browning meats and sauce reduction
- 26cm crepe pan
- 24cm omelette pan
- shallow vegetable roasting trays
- deep meat roasting tray

> **TIP** : *Some milk pans have pouring lips on both sides – ideal for those who are left handed.*

NON-STICK COATED COOKWARE

Non-stick pans have come a long way and those available today bear little resemblance to what we used to buy. They can be amazingly durable – but having said that, a good non-stick pan will only ever last if it is taken care of, and that means using the correct cooking temperature and the right utensils.

Of course the great advantages of a non-stick pan are that there is a reduced risk of food sticking and less oil or fat is required in the pan – which naturally makes for healthier cooking and eating.

My favourite non-stick pans are stainless steel with a heavy-gauge aluminium or copper core and a stainless steel base.

- 20cm shallow skillet, for eggs and crepes
- 30cm wok pan

COPPER PANS

Professional copper pans are possibly the most expensive you can buy and are considered to be the best by many chefs for their fast and even heat transfer.

Traditionally the pans are solid, heavy-gauge copper (as opposed to plated) and lined with tin or nickel to prevent food reactions occurring. As tin and nickel can wear through however, modern copper pans are made from about 90% copper and lined with 18/10 stainless steel.

Plated copper cookware gives the look of solid copper but is usually stainless steel with a thin, copper-plated exterior.

STOCK POTS

A stock or pasta pot is essential for making stock, soup and a reasonable amount of pasta. A tall narrow stock pot with a lid means less evaporation. Around 10 litre capacity is a useful size.

My favourite stock pot is a stainless steel, multi-function pot rather than a conventional stock pot. A colander insert sits neatly inside the pot during cooking so pasta can be easily drained without having to carry the whole pot to the sink. With the lid on, it can also be used for steaming vegetables, which saves you having to buy and store a separate steamer.

> **TIP** : *For easier cleaning, choose pans with a stainless steel outer base rather than copper or aluminium.*

FRY PANS

My everyday fry pan or skillet is made from stainless steel with an inner core of copper. It's reasonably light, easy to clean and so versatile I use it for everything from browning meats to frying eggs.

Sauté pans have a wide flat base with straight, deep sides and a lid. They are perfect for sauce reduction and for browning foods like onions and meats (which then require prolonged cooking). The best sauté pans are suitable for stove top as well as oven use, and are heavy based to conduct heat evenly. A really useful pan is around 26cm in diameter in either stainless steel (with an aluminium or copper core in the sides and base), hard-anodised aluminium or lined copper.

> **TIP** : *Use a spatter cover to prevent oil or sauce from making a mess.*

Iron char grill pans are an excellent, quick and easy indoor alternative to an outdoor barbeque. Grills with raised ridges give fish, meats and even toasted bread a lovely char-grilled pattern, and they also help to drain away excess fat. Smooth grills can be used for cooking pancakes or eggs and are relatively easy to store.

I find handles aren't necessary but some models are sold with them if you prefer. Single or double size grills will sit neatly over one or two elements on gas, electric and even ceramic cook tops and can be moved directly into the oven if necessary. New cast iron does require initial seasoning but over time develops a patina which provides an excellent non-stick surface.

Deep frying can be done in a high-sided, heavy-based sauce-pan but if you're seriously into fried foods, you may prefer to buy an enamelled steel chip fryer, specially suited for the job.

A *wok* is useful but not essential – unless of course you prepare a lot of Asian foods or stir-fries. A new wok must be seasoned like any pressed steel pot and will frequently have a sticky coating when you buy it new. Woks are also available with non-stick coatings or made from cast iron.

ENAMELLED CAST IRON COOKING POTS

For slow-cooking dishes like risotto, soups, curry and stews, I love using enamelled cast iron pots and use them nearly every day purely for their versatility. I cook just about everything in them and now have several in various sizes.

They're great for frying onions and vegetables, and I also like to brown meat directly on top of the stove, then place the whole pot – lid and all – into the oven. They look so good I even present the food in them directly at the table.

Cast iron takes on the heat slowly but distributes it evenly across the surface making it a very efficient though heavy material. It's extremely tolerant of high heats, withstands deforming and is suitable for all heat sources and stove tops. These pots are expensive but, in my opinion, well worth the investment. Cared for, they will last a lifetime and are a great gift for anyone starting a home. Buy them one at a time if you need to, until you have a set which will cover the cooking needs of your household.

My favourite enamelled cast iron pots:

- 20cm round Dutch oven
- 24cm round Dutch oven
- 32cm bistro pan

> **TIP** : *Clay pots are perfect for cooking slowly in the oven. I use mine mainly for rice, which it cooks to absolute perfection.*

Prepare

When time is short and hungry family and friends are ready to descend,
the secret in the kitchen is to be prepared. Having the right basic
equipment not only saves time but also helps you to stay calm and
at least appear confident that everything is completely under control!

FOOD PREPARATION

Every kitchen needs a good basic selection of cookware. This will not only make your food simpler to serve but also make it easier to prepare and perhaps even make it taste better!

Of course, it's all too easy to accumulate all sorts of gadgets and appliances, but filling your kitchen cupboards and drawers with things you rarely use does not make good sense – it only makes it hard to find what you're looking for. And who needs hold-ups at meal preparation time?

I want to share with you what every well-equipped kitchen should have and what appliances and utensils are most important. So have a good look in your kitchen and take stock of what you do and don't need. Have that clean out! For the effort, both you and your cupboards will breathe a huge sigh of relief. You can then concentrate on getting the things that will prove the most useful. You'll be surprised at what a difference it makes next time you're in the kitchen whipping up a meal.

TIP : Sort kitchen utensils into groups. Store them in attractive jars on the bench or hanging from racks for great display and easy everyday access.

CHECKLIST

ESSENTIALS

- Knives & sharpening stone
- Chopping boards
- Set of stainless steel bowls
- Spoons – wooden & metal
- Hand whisk
- Kitchen fork
- Sieve
- Spatulas
- Peeler
- Scissors
- Graters
- Cheese plane
- Juicer
- Zester
- Potato masher
- Fish slice
- Tongs
- Scales
- Timer
- Measuring spoons, cups & jug
- Tea towels

GOOD TO HAVE

- Set of glass mixing bowls
- Garlic press
- Kitchen & meat thermometers
- Pepper mill
- Mortar & pestle
- Ice-cream scoop
- Soup ladle
- Salad spinner
- Pastry brushes
- Rolling pin

KNIVES

Anyone who has ever had the misfortune to suffer a bad knife will share my joy in a blade so sharp it cuts like butter. A decent knife is such an important part of any kitchen that I urge you to invest as much as you can possibly afford and buy at least one very good one. Don't even bother with the cheap supermarket varieties, unless of course you plan to take one on your next fishing trip!

WHAT TO LOOK FOR IN A KNIFE

- High-carbon stainless steel knives are my choice. With proper care, they will last forever and rarely need sharpening. Resistant to rust and staining, they can be used for acidic foods without reaction.
- The best knives are forged rather than stamped. A forged blade will be evenly balanced and have a tapered cutting edge. This strengthens the knife and allows greater control.
- A good knife should always be weighted in the handle. This is often referred to as the 'tang' – the section of the blade that extends past the bolster and can often be seen between the two sides of the handle.
- For long-term durability, I prefer knives with solid stainless steel or wooden handles rather than plastic or synthetic.
- If funds are short, start with one good cook's knife and one paring knife.

KNIFE CARE

- Store knives in separate drawer compartments or in a block. If space is at a premium, a simple sleeve of thick cardboard can be made to protect the blades between uses.
- Use only wooden or polyethylene chopping boards. Glass, granite or metal will damage the cutting edge.
- Avoid placing knives in the dishwasher. Wash and dry them well by hand after each use and return them to their storage as soon as possible. Do not allow wooden handles to soak in water.

CUTTING & SLICING ESSENTIALS

COOK'S KNIFE

- This is the knife I would choose above all others. It is suitable for slicing just about anything, from great chunks of meat to fine, delicate herbs.
- A good cook's knife has a wide blade designed to cope with repeated impact against a chopping board.
- The pointy end will look after the lighter cutting, and the heel (or heavy end) will slice through even the toughest pumpkin.
- Select a blade around 20–25cm in length.

BREAD KNIFE

- The bread knife has a long serrated blade that cuts through bread or any other soft food with a tough crust or skin.
- It is not suitable for cutting meat as the serrated edge will make a jagged cut.

TOMATO/SANDWICH KNIFE

- A smaller knife with a serrated blade, this is wonderful for slicing tomatoes.

PARING KNIFE

- A miniature version of the cook's knife. Around 10cm long, it is perfect for delicate slicing or peeling of small fruits and vegetables, garlic and ginger.

MEZZALUNA

- While it's not strictly a knife, a mezzaluna is a wonderful tool. It has a crescent-shaped blade and is one of my favourites for quick chopping.
- Use on a wooden chopping board by rocking the blade over the food to chop it finely – perfect for herbs, garlic and onions.

SCISSORS

- So useful for quickly snipping herbs, bacon, even pastry or string.
- Look for stainless steel, easy-clean blades and use them only in the kitchen. Wash thoroughly between uses.

> **TIP** : *A blunt knife can be more dangerous than a sharp one as more pressure needs to be exerted to cut. Keep blades as sharp as possible by using a steel or stone on a regular basis.*

CHOPPING BOARDS

Wooden boards are just so nice to use that I rarely want any other kind. A set of four in varying sizes with one reserved just for raw meat is a great start.

Keep them clean by scrubbing with warm, soapy water and a stiff brush and never allow them to stand in pools of water or they may split.

ESSENTIAL UTENSILS

GARLIC PRESS

Garlic can be crushed with the heel of a cook's knife or using a pestle and mortar but I find a garlic press to be invaluable. It should be easy to clean and preferably dishwasher safe.

PEELER

My favourite peelers are the little plastic ones with the curved 'beak' at the front for picking the eyes from potatoes.

WOODEN SPOONS

I store my wooden spoons in a vase by the stove and they look so tempting to use that I always have about three on the go while I'm cooking. Start with a few in different sizes and lengths and use separate ones for sweet and savoury.

METAL SPOONS

A large metal spoon with a long handle is ideal for basting. You'll also need a slotted one for draining.

SOUP LADLE

A good, generously sized ladle is a must when cooking soups and stocks. A cooking ladle is rather long handled, while a serving ladle has a little more 'table appeal'.

HAND WHISK

A whisk is a real boon for lump-free white sauce, custard and gravy or for beating eggs.

SPATULAS

Flexible rubber heads on wooden handles are perfect for scraping the pan clean. For hot sauces in pans, look for the newer silicone heads which will withstand high temperatures.

KITCHEN FORK

Essential for holding roasted meat while carving.

FISH SLICE

Not for slicing fish at all but rather for sliding under foods to prevent them from sticking whilst cooking. My mother used to have the best slice. It was long, thin bladed and flexible, all the things you are looking for when lifting delicate foods like fried eggs – and even fillets of fish!

TONGS

An absolute essential in my house, I'm completely lost without my tongs. I have one or two pairs, plus a long-handled pair for the barbeque.

POTATO MASHER

You can get by with a fork, but for big mashing jobs, a masher is a must. Never be fooled into thinking a food processor can mash your potatoes – hand mashing is hard to beat for texture.

ICE-CREAM SCOOP

Any way you serve it, ice-cream is always good!

OVEN MITTS AND CLOTHS

Keep these within easy reach of the stove or oven. Either thick fabric or the new silicone mitts will help protect your hands from hot containers.

PEPPER MILL

For the best flavour, freshly cracked pepper always wins hands down. Invest in a good quality wooden mill.

TEA TOWELS

Both linen and cotton are natural, highly absorbent fibres which can be boiled and washed over and over. Have a few specifically for food preparation and keep the others for general kitchen use.

APRONS

For grubs like me who always seem to spoil their good clothes when cooking an old-fashioned apron is a must. Cotton is light-weight and easy to throw in the wash.

MORTAR AND PESTLE

Ideal for crushing and pulverising anything from fresh garlic to dried spices and salt. Lots of flavour – and lots of fun too!

PASTRY BRUSHES

Wonderful for applying oil or marinades to fish, meat and vegetables, and for greasing pans. Wash them by hand.

HAND JUICER

A hand juicer is all you need for one or two pieces of fruit. Plastic types are widely available but you may prefer an old-style glass juicer or even a contemporary metal one.

STAINLESS STEEL BOWLS

A nest of bowls is not only incredibly useful but also easy to store. Stainless steel is the best choice as highly acidic foods can react with other metals.

GLASS BOWLS

Pyrex bowls can be used to mix ingredients or microwave vegetables and will withstand both boiling hot and icy cold liquids. Perfect for marinades and overnight food storage in the fridge, these bowls are incredibly strong and hard wearing. Purchase in an assortment of sizes and stack them inside each other to save kitchen storage space.

COLANDERS

Essential for draining and washing food. Choose a good sized bowl with adequate drainage holes. For durability, opt for metal rather than plastic. Stainless steel or enamel coated are good choices. Make sure the colander has strong handles or wide rims for easy gripping.

STRAINERS AND SIEVES

Conical stainless steel strainers are intended for sauce making but can also be used for general straining. A finer, flatter wire mesh sieve is good for sifting flour as well as straining. Buy metal rather than plastic and select styles that fit over your most-used bowls and jugs.

SALAD SPINNER

For dressings to coat salad leaves properly, they must be dried well after washing. This can be done with a clean, dry tea cloth, but a salad spinner, while not truly essential, works brilliantly and is a real time saver.

GRATERS AND CHEESE PLANE

Box graters are 'great' for cheese and vegetables. The handle on top allows you to press down firmly while the four sides each provide a different texture.

Fine or coarse micro-plane graters are perfect for nuts, ginger, citrus peel and parmesan, while a cheese plane is terrific when making sandwiches. This neat tool makes slicing cheese so easy. It works well on medium to firm cheeses which aren't too crumbly.

ZESTER

Recipes often call for citrus zest and this little tool removes only the fragrant outer layer of the skin, leaving behind the bitter white pith.

Once you have one you'll wonder how you ever got by in the kitchen without it!

Bake

I remember a comment made by a friend many years ago about his new wife. 'She bakes,' he said with immense pride. Now coming from anyone else, I wouldn't have paid much attention. But he was incredibly 'cool' and hardly the type, I thought, to enjoy anything from a home kitchen rather than a chic café. I take pleasure therefore in the fact that my love of baking is 'cool' and that the results hopefully please others as much as my friend's wife's pleased him!

ESSENTIALS

- [ ] Cake tins & trays
- [ ] Measuring cups
- [ ] Measuring spoons
- [ ] Measuring jug
- [ ] Timer
- [ ] Scales
- [ ] Set of mixing bowls
- [ ] Sieves
- [ ] Cooling rack
- [ ] Storage tins/tubs
- [ ] Baking paper
- [ ] Plastic wrap
- [ ] Storage tubs & jars
- [ ] Roasting trays with racks
- [ ] Shallow roasting trays
- [ ] Rectangular gratin dish
- [ ] Porcelain ramekins
- [ ] Aluminium foil

GOOD TO HAVE

- [ ] Cooking thermometer
- [ ] Rolling pin
- [ ] Pastry brush
- [ ] Pallet knife
- [ ] Cutters & icing equipment
- [ ] Oil atomiser

ROASTING AND BAKING

If I had to choose, one of my favourite meals is a good roast dinner. And I'll happily admit I cook them often. Plenty of crunchy, golden potatoes. Heaps of steaming gravy. There is simply no comfort food like it.

And surely roasting is one of the easiest, most hassle-free ways to cook. A few minutes of preparation and the rest is left to the oven. Particularly on a Sunday, what can be more satisfying than a delicious meal, dessert or cake cooking away by itself leaving you time to do other things?

From many years of the Sunday roast experience, I have realised not only the value of the freshest ingredients, but also the advantages of having an astute selection of baking tins and pans.

Home baked food is one of life's simpler, shared joys. And the smell throughout the house as it's baking is heavenly. Need I tempt you further with the thought of scrumptious treats — sweet or savoury — straight out of the oven and into your mouth?

> **TIP** : *For spontaneous home baking, keep a few basic ingredients on hand — like flour, sugar, butter and eggs. Then you can whip up a treat just about anytime!*

CAKE TINS

While aluminium tins and trays are fine, heavier steel or stainless steel are the ones which will truly last.

TO STICK OR NOT TO STICK

Heavy gauge non-stick muffin and biscuit trays are useful, but for sponge and fruit cakes, I prefer uncoated steel or stainless steel. Baking a sponge cake in non-stick pans is tempting for easy turn-out but results in a cake with a dark, shiny and crisp crust. You can prevent this by greasing and lining the tins with patty pan cases or baking paper. I use this method for all tins and trays regardless of them being uncoated or non-stick.

> **TIP** : *To prevent steel tins from rusting after washing, place them in a warm oven to thoroughly dry before putting them back in the cupboard.*

MY MOST USEFUL CAKE TINS AND TRAYS

- *Round 20cm*, uncoated stainless steel × 2 for layer cakes.

- *Square 18cm*, uncoated stainless steel × 2 for sponges.

- *Square 22cm*, for chocolate brownies.

- *Slice 20cm x 30cm*, non-stick for slices and slab cakes.

- *Springform 20cm*, non-stick. Springform tins have a buckle which when unclipped allows the collar of the pan to be lifted away from the base. This is especially good for easy removal of fragile desserts like cheesecake.

- *Biscuit and cookie sheets* The best are made from heavy steel but I have quite a few now ranging from stainless steel to non-stick aluminium.

- *Muffin pan, 12-cup*, uncoated stainless steel or heavy non-stick. Even with a non-stick pan, I prefer to use paper muffin pan cases for easy removal.

- *Mini patty cake pan, 12-cup*, uncoated stainless steel or heavy non-stick. I use these for fairy or butterfly cakes, even savoury starters. I grease the individual pans well and also use patty pan cases or circles of baking paper.

- *Bread or loaf pans 10cm x 20cm*, deep, heavy uncoated steel. Mine have folded and pleated corners which in my opinion produce a nicer looking cake or loaf than the newer curved style.

- *Pyrex* A deep glass baking dish is good for both sweet and savoury dishes. I like mine for fruit pies and crumbles. Unlike some metals, glass won't react to acidic fruits and can be used safely to store any left-overs in the fridge for several days. Don't forget to cover them with cling film or a lid.

> **TIP** : *There is a general rule when baking cakes in square tins, that is if the recipe calls for, say, a round pan of 20cm but you want to use a square tin, you need to go down one size or around 2cm. Therefore you will need a square tin of 18cm.*

BAKING ESSENTIALS

MEASURING CUPS

For dry foods like flour and sugar. Buy them in sets.

MEASURING SPOONS

Never guess a spoon measurement. Accuracy is the key to successful baking.

MEASURING JUG

For liquid measures, a large glass Pyrex jug will withstand both hot and cold temperatures.

KITCHEN SCALES

A removable bowl is helpful and saves time when baking. Try to buy a set which shows both metric and imperial. I prefer a needle and dial to digital, mainly for looks but also they don't require batteries!

KITCHEN THERMOMETER

Invaluable when making sugar syrups, jams and toffees.

SET OF MIXING BOWLS

For a fabulous display, as well as practicality, buy bowls which nest inside one another. I prefer round or oval glazed ceramic – the best for 'hugging' the bowl while you're beating.

SIEVES

Sieving is essential to eliminate lumps and incorporate air into the dry ingredients when making cakes. Avoid plastic and have a couple in different mesh sizes for flour and icing sugar.

WIRE COOLING RACKS

For cooling hot, turned out baked goods before serving or storing. The raised rack will allow steam to escape while the grids should be fairly close to each other to reduce damage to the surface of the cake.

SPOONS

For scooping and folding in dry ingredients, metal spoons are the best, but for mixing, I like to use medium length wooden spoons. Keep a couple of wooden spoons just for baking as wood is porous and tends to absorb and transfer strong flavours like onion or garlic.

SPATULA

Unless you or your kids love to lick the bowl, you'll need a spatula for scraping out every last yummy drop!

PALLET KNIFE

This broad, flat bladed knife is so useful for spreading icing, frosting, whipped cream and melted chocolate.

PASTRY BRUSH

Perfect for applying beaten egg or milk to achieve a crisp, golden crust on pies, scones, buns and loaves of bread.

CUTTERS

Fun for kids and grown ups too. Wash and dry them well to prevent rusting.

ROLLING PIN

A long wooden pin without handles is my pick for pastry and icing.

ICING EQUIPMENT

Even just a bag with a few nozzles will have you prepared for any birthday cake.

TIMER

A cake has to be timed exactly. Make sure the ring is loud.

BAKING PAPER

Essential for lining tins to prevent cakes and biscuits from sticking. Buy in rolls from your supermarket.

BAKING TRAYS AND DISHES

A good roasting pan will cook meat and vegetables to perfection while still being comfortable enough to hold and fit inside your oven. Quality is the key here. The pan needs to be sturdy enough to cope with the highest of temperatures without buckling, but also relatively easy to keep clean.

Select a size according to your needs. Consider the amount of meat and vegetables you would roast for a normal occasion. Keep in mind too that a large roast in a small pan will cook unevenly and a small roast in a large pan will result in the juices spreading thinly and burning. Pans should be rigid, with sides high enough to restrict splattering. And since roasts can be heavy, a pan with handles or flat rims will allow you to grip and carry it easily.

Some roasting pans come with lids and racks, which makes for much more versatile baking and braising. A rack will raise meat above the juices, allowing a crisper crust to form. A lid is very useful for slower cooking as it helps to retain moisture. Alternatively, you can always cover an unlidded pan with aluminium foil.

Roasting pans can take up more than their fair share of storage space, so to minimise this either stand them on their sides or stack them within one another – even inside the oven when it's not in use.

Before you go shopping for new roasting and baking trays, carefully check the measurements of your oven and jot them down. It's far too easy to be seduced by a beautiful big pan, only to find it won't fit in your oven once you get it home.

My favourite roasting pans :
- 30cm x 36cm deep stainless steel with handles and removable rack
- hard-anodised, non-stick, deep meat roasting tray with handles
- hard-anodised, non-stick, shallow vegetable roasting trays
- commercial quality aluminium shallow roasting trays
- 26cm x 40cm enamelled cast iron oven dish

ROASTING EQUIPMENT

- *Rectangular gratin dish.* One of these glazed, ceramic dishes is essential for baking meals like lasagne. Suitable for freezer-to-oven use, rectangular as opposed to oval is easier to store in both the cupboard and fridge and takes up less room in the oven.
- *Porcelain ramekins.* Essential for baking little custards and my favourite, crème brûlée. Most desserts like this call for the ramekins to be placed in a roasting pan of water to about halfway up the sides.
- *Meat thermometer.* Vital for ensuring tender roasted meats that have been cooked for just the right amount of time.
- *Aluminium foil.* To cover meat or other dishes during cooking to prevent further browning and burning.
- *Basting spoon.* A long handle makes basting juices a little safer.
- *Oil brush.* Extremely useful for brushing oil, marinades and syrups onto meats, fish, vegetables and fruits.
- *Oil atomiser.* Great to have because it means you use less oil when cooking.

Kitchen appliances

The temptation of shiny new gadgets is often hard to resist, but try to only buy

appliances you know will be truly useful.

CHECKLIST

ESSENTIALS
   Toaster
   Kettle
   Electric hand mixer
   Immersion blender

GOOD TO HAVE
   Benchtop or stand mixer
   Food processor
   Bar blender
   Coffee press or plunger
   Coffee percolator
   Coffee grinder
   Juice extractor
   Electric citrus juicer

SHOPPING FOR KITCHEN APPLIANCES

Most kitchens should have the essentials like a kettle and toaster, but other appliances will only ever be valuable if they save time and effort on a regular basis and can justify their cupboard or bench space. I'm only too aware that the temptation of shiny new gadgets can be hard to resist, but you should try to limit your selection to the ones that are going to be the work-horses of the kitchen. You can take some of the guesswork out of this by taking the time to consider the sorts of things you usually cook and how you prefer to prepare them.

When shopping for new appliances, look for styles which coordinate with your kitchen and are easy to maintain and keep clean. They should be as versatile as possible too, and have the capacity to perform well over many years of sustained use. Appliances with the most power and capacity will handle extra demands when needed and will generally last the longest. Regular cleaning or wiping down after every use and before storing is a great way to preserve their longevity. And if you have small children in the household, look at the safety aspects of kitchen appliances too.

TIP : *Design an appliance shelf or cupboard for easy use and storage.*

TOASTER

The once-humble pop-up toaster has really come into its own as a kitchen fashion statement. Many modern styles have a curved 'retro' appearance in bold colours or stainless steel. These look great and most of us would be happy to leave them on permanent display.

Pop-up toasters are generally available in 2 or 4 slice models and an extra lift lever is helpful for removing those left-over crusty bits. Extra wide slots are essential for toasting bagels or muffins. Adjustable settings allow you to select browning and a cancel button saves burning while a slide-out crumb tray helps with cleaning.

If you're bold, go for colour – it can add a real style 'accent' to your kitchen. But if you prefer the look of stainless steel, a satin or brushed finish will be easier to maintain than chrome.

KETTLE

I just would not survive without a cup of tea in the morning!

A good electric kettle will boil 2 cups of water in around 2 minutes and should hold at least 1.5L or 6 cups of water. Cordless kettles with a swivel base offer greater convenience and re-filling is easier when the lid is wide and removable.

An automatic shut-off switch is essential; a water level indicator is very useful. Illuminated switches show when the power is off or on. The element should be stainless steel. Removable filters prevent particles going into the cup.

TIP : A coffee press can also be used for tea but do buy a separate pot so the flavours don't mix.

FRENCH COFFEE PRESS OR PLUNGER

The French press or plunger is a design classic. The lid has an in-built filter which is pushed down to hold back the coffee grounds from the brew. A glass container allows you to see the coffee level easily. A domed chrome lid is more stylish and stain resistant than plastic and the built-in mesh filter means you won't need filter papers. Sizes vary from 2 cups to 12 cups.

TIP : Have an extra pastry brush to remove excess coffee powder from your grinder after each use. Bean oils can turn rancid if allowed to build up.

PERCOLATORS

I like stove percolators purely for their looks, but they also happen to make good coffee. You fill the pot with water and coffee and place it on the stove. As it heats up, the water is forced up through the central tube and over the coffee. Percolators like this are available in different sizes, but I'm happy with mine which makes coffee just for one!

COFFEE GRINDERS

Grinding your own beans will give the best coffee flavour. Small electric grinders or mills, depending on how particular you are about your grind, are relatively inexpensive. The best grinders will give an evenly textured grind with very little dust. Mills keep the beans cooler and therefore retain more flavour. A burr mill is considered to be better but will cost more.

If you're going to go to the trouble of grinding your own beans, remember to buy freshly roasted beans and grind only the amount you need just before using them.

IMMERSION BLENDER

I really enjoy cooking rustic foods and often make my own tomato-based pasta sauces and soupy stews. For this kind of cooking I like a little texture and a hand-held blender is often all I need to use. A blender like this can be plunged directly into a pot of sauce and then rinsed straight off under the tap. A real favourite of the lazy cook!

> **TIP** : *Take care when plunging an immersion blender into hot liquids and sauces. Blades should be fully submerged to prevent splashing. Take the pot off the stove first.*

Hand blenders come with various attachments and containers for blending as well as chopping. A three-cup chopper bowl is a good size for nuts, cooked meats and herbs.

Cordless blenders are convenient but less powerful – and let's face it, who needs another gadget that needs re-charging? I suggest one with a long power cord instead.

To be useful, the minimum power should be around 200 watts and blades should be stainless steel. Shafts need to be long enough to go into deep pots and should have a splash guard.

Look for an easy-wipe body and check that cups and blades are dishwasher proof.

BENCHTOP OR STAND MIXER

Every serious cook dreams of having a hands-free mixer that gets on with the work of heavy duty beating, mixing and whipping while they are free to get on with something else.

When choosing a mixer, a higher wattage doesn't necessarily mean that it has more power – it all comes down to the design, how the attachments move and how much flour or dough it can handle. To measure a stand mixer's power, look for the term 'flour power'. Six cups should be the minimum, but for heavy dough mixing go for at least 10–20 cups.

The best stand mixers operate with 'planetary action' where the beater rotates around its own axis. This gives it more contact with the ingredients and reduces the need to keep stopping the machine to scrape down the mixture.

The best machines have several attachments including a flat beater for mixing cake batters, a dough hook for mixing and kneading yeast doughs, and a wire whisk or whip for beating air into egg whites or cream. Some even have attachments for making pasta dough, grinding or mincing meat, and juicing citrus fruits.

A good benchtop mixer will weigh around 10 kilos – heavy enough to prevent it from creeping along the bench while it's operating.

HAND-HELD ELECTRIC MIXER

If you have limited space, only bake occasionally, or don't need to mix heavy doughs, then a hand-held electric mixer is a perfect alternative to a stand mixer. They mix and whip, just a like a stand mixer, only with less power. Purely for their convenience though, I do think every kitchen needs one. They can be easily stored away in a cupboard or drawer, and because they're also portable, you can mix directly into any pans and bowls as needed.

The best hand mixers have a strong motor which is powerful enough to mix a heavy batter or cake mix without slowing down or stopping. The minimum power should be around 175 watts, but a high wattage doesn't always indicate high power.

The design of the beaters also affects performance. Old-style hand-held mixers are heavier and chrome plated with thick posts down the centres. The new designs are made from stainless steel wire and are lighter, more efficient and easier to clean. Removable beaters and whisks can be used without clogging for all lightweight mixing jobs like batters, cake mixes, cream and eggs.

The best hand mixers have at least six speeds plus a 'soft' or 'slow start' button which saves great clouds of flour dust or sprays of batter escaping from the bowl.

> **TIP** : *A wall mount is useful, but hand-held mixers can also be stored neatly in a drawer.*

FOOD PROCESSOR

I don't consider a food processor to be totally essential but if you like to cook or have a big family to prepare for, definitely consider one because they can save so much time in chopping and mixing.

Often, the more expensive food processors will be the most powerful and my advice is to select a machine with a robust motor of around 950 watts. Look for several power options as well as a 'pulse' switch to quickly turn the machine on and off for crushing ice or mixing tough loads like pastries and heavy dough.

Food processors are sold according to their dry ingredient capacity and this can vary from 1 to around 20 cups. A capacity of less than 5 cups is useful for chopping small things, like say an onion or nuts, but is just too small for most jobs. I would suggest a larger size of at least 9–16 cups, and some of these larger models come with a 4 cup mini bowl which fits inside the main bowl for those smaller jobs. If you need to regularly prepare a lot of food, then don't hesitate in buying a professional size of around 20 cups.

A clear polycarbonate bowl will be the most stain resistant and durable and the lid should have the widest feed tube available. Take my word for it, you don't want to have to pre-cut every vegetable just to fit it down the tube – it takes far too much time.

I like to use the stainless steel blades for general chopping, the cutting discs for slicing and shredding, and the plastic hook for mixing pastry dough.

Some processors even have blender and juicer attachments which make the whole machine a lot more versatile and space efficient.

Some also come with a whipping attachment for cake mixes, eggs and cream, but for those I still prefer to use my hand-held electric or stand mixers as they incorporate more air and seem to do a better job.

BAR BLENDER

A blender is permanently plugged in at my house for blending fruit into smoothies, pureeing vegetables into soups and crushing ice for drinks. I find it blends more smoothly than a food processor. If you can't have both, buy a food processor with a blender attachment or a hand-held blender instead.

The best quality blenders use around 350–500 watts and have up to five speeds, including ice crushing plus a 'pulse' button. A pulse function keeps ingredients moving. The container should hold around 4–7 cups. I prefer tempered glass to stainless steel so I can see what's going on.

The base should be wide and heavy. Around 3–5 kilos will help prevent it from bouncing when pureeing really thick foods. The blades should be made of stainless steel. Rubber or plastic seals should always be used to stop leaks. Make sure the lid seals tightly and has a removable section for adding extra ingredients and allowing steam to escape when blending hot liquids.

> **TIP** : *To clean the blender jar, add hot water and a few drops of dishwashing liquid and run it for a few seconds.*

ELECTRIC CITRUS JUICERS

Electric juicers are good if you juice larger amounts of citrus fruits on a regular basis.

The best models have die-cast bases, run at around 100–150 watts and have a reamer cone which is strong and sharp enough to juice well.

The juicer needs to be able to handle both small and large citrus fruit sizes, and a reversible function will allow more juice to be extracted from the fruit.

Some styles also strain the pulp and pips from the juice and have a clear bowl for better visibility, along with a pouring lip and fluid level measure.

JUICE EXTRACTOR

Fresh fruit and vegetable juices are such a delicious way to incorporate more vitamins and minerals into your diet and having your own juicer is a convenient and affordable way to consume them every day. Even kids who usually turn their noses up at anything vaguely green or orange are now catching on to the craze set up by chic shopping centre juice bars. Having a juicer and a bar blender as well will mean you can whip up exotic mixes with ice and yoghurt too. You and yours will be brimming with good health in no time!

Juicers aren't easy to clean or store so you really need to be a dedicated juice lover in order to get the full benefit. You should also take into consideration the storage space required for the fruit and vegetables as a reasonable amount is often needed just to make one jug of juice.

A large feed tube requires less pre-chopping of fruits and vegetables, while a large pulp container lets you continue juicing longer before emptying. Alternatively, you could consider a commercial pulp-ejection juicer that directs the waste out of the machine and into a separate container. Try not to throw the pulp into the bin – it makes great compost!

When shopping for a juice extractor, make sure disks, filters and containers will be easy to clean. Go for power of around 1000 watts to give you the most juice possible. Variable speed controls allow you to juice both hard and soft foodstuffs.

It might be worth your while buying a book or two of juicing 'recipes' as well. There are plenty available, and most discuss the specific health benefits of various fruits and vegetables. But do experiment a little to come up with your own nutritious favourites!

My favourite daily juice :
- 4 x carrots, cleaned and peeled
- 2 x green apples, cored and de-seeded
- 2 x celery stalks
- 1 piece of fresh ginger, peeled
- A squeeze of fresh lemon or lime juice

If time allows, I place this juice mixture into my bar blender and blend with one cup of crushed iced for a refreshing twist.

> **TIP** : *For easier cleaning, line the pulp catcher with recycled plastic bags. The pulp can then be easily disposed of or poured into the compost*

Kitchen storage

The kitchen easily has the potential to become the most cluttered
room in the house so ample storage and good organisation are vital.
Even if space is limited, establishing a system incorporating creative
storage ideas will make all the difference between order and chaos.

STORAGE EFFICIENCY

For a kitchen to operate smoothly and efficiently, regular cleaning and sorting of the cupboards and drawers is needed – to prevent things getting out of hand. This will allow you to see what you have and assess what you no longer use. Then you can make some clear space for those new items which you do need.

To establish an efficient work space, it's a good idea to start by having a thorough clear out. Stack everything to one side and wash down shelves and inside drawers with warm, soapy water. While the cupboards are drying, re-organise things into groups according to their use. For the sake of hygiene as much as anything else, broken or damaged items should be disposed of and replaced as necessary. Check the food items in your pantry too, as these should be rotated frequently and used to prevent waste. This will also give you a good idea of what items need replenishing. Open packages should be sealed or their contents transferred into airtight containers to keep them fresh. Foodstuffs past their use-by dates should be discarded.

TIP : *If cupboard space is limited, consider installing strong wall shelves for pots, plates, cups and glassware.*

CHECKLIST

ESSENTIALS

- Cupboards
- Drawers
- Containers
- Jars
- Bottles
- Bags and wraps

GOOD TO HAVE

- Recipe files
- Cooking magazine holders
- Baskets with lids

CUPBOARDS

It's important to have basic order in each cupboard and the discipline to ensure that when something is used, it goes back to exactly the same place. Now if everyone in the family knows this – and acts on it! – then your frustration at never being able to find things should be a thing of the past.

Sort cupboards into :

- food and pantry items
- plates and bowls
- glasses and cups
- pots and pans
- baking tins and trays
- storage containers
- serving platters and dishes
- small appliances

DRAWERS

Deep drawers, instead of cupboards, are the way forward in modern kitchens – and rightly so, as things are so much easier to see and find.

Line drawers with washable grip mat to prevent things from sliding around, and avoid scratching and chipping stacked plates by cutting circles of felt to place between each.

Insert trays will keep everything in order, while soft-close runners will prevent trapped fingers.

> **TIP** : *Drawers on either side of the stove can be used for utensils, spices or oven gloves.*

STORAGE CONTAINERS

To prevent spoiling and contamination, left-over food should be stored in airtight containers, jars, zip-lock bags or under plastic wrap in a cool cupboard or refrigerator. Quality food containers will last so much longer than cheaper varieties and can go safely into the freezer, microwave or dishwasher. Remember that not all are food safe, especially in the microwave, so you should only use those which state this clearly on the label.

Use clear containers for easy viewing of the contents. For neat stacking and storage, lids should be flat and the containers straight sided. Lids must be firm fitting and easy to snap on and off. Airtight containers are essential in preventing dried foodstuffs from turning stale.

All-purpose plastic boxed sets in a variety of sizes are ideal for storing small and large amounts food in the fridge or cupboard. A lettuce crisper will lengthen the fridge life of lettuces and cabbages. Cereal boxes with wide-pour lids save time and mess in the morning and help retain freshness.

> **TIP** : *Wash and dry plastic containers well and store with lids off to prevent odours.*

For cakes and cookies, I like to line the containers with silicone or brown paper to prevent sticking and absorb moisture. Keep an eye out at garage sales and markets for interesting old biscuit and cake tins. They are not only perfect for storing your home-baked goodies, but will look terrific on your kitchen bench. It will be hard to keep fingers away from the lids!

BOTTLES AND JARS

Recycled jars make perfect storage for all sorts of things. Clear wine bottles are perfect for serving chilled water.

BAGS AND WRAPS

Use snap-lock bags for storing dry ingredients and freezing left-over wine and easy-thaw portions of meat.

Purchase plastic wraps in bulk catering sizes to save both money and time. Use only brands which are microwave oven and food safe. Aluminium foil is best avoided for storing as it may react with some salty foods or acids like lemon juice, vinegar or tomatoes.

Baking paper can be used to wrap food for added freshness when storing.

eat

Meal times are important in my house and for dinner at the very least, we always sit down around a table to eat.

A roast on Sundays is almost an institution! Busy weeknights can be a challenge but are by no means less important. As a way of unwinding from the day, the preparing of simple meals is something we look forward to. Traditions like this encourage conversation and a definite sense of togetherness.

Furnish for eating

Enjoying good food and company is surely one of life's true pleasures
but I'm not a real believer in setting up a room especially for dining.
I prefer to set up an area for eating right in the hub of things, somewhere
the kids can do their homework, games can be played and snacks or main
meals can be enjoyed with ease and a sense of togetherness. The space you have
available will of course dictate the shape and size of your furniture but it's just
so important to have one central meeting point where everyone can come
together, even if only briefly to enjoy food and each other's laughter.

SHOPPING FOR A TABLE

For a table style which won't date, choose clean lines with a slight taper in the legs. Highly stylised carving, the shape and material are what can age a table the most so go for classic elegance where possible. Ideally it should seat all of your household comfortably, with the possible addition of a friend or two.

A table too 'good' or highly polished will never be enjoyed or used as much as one which can take a few knocks. It's far better to choose user-friendly finishes rather than having to cover a beautiful table in a swathe of blankets just to protect it.

A rustic, wooden table is ideal for daily use as the surface will take all sorts of wear without causing too much grief. More highly polished styles will need mats to protect the surface from heat and scratching. Glass, stone and marble, while being extremely durable can be cold and appear unwelcoming.

Round tables are a practical shape in high-traffic areas, whereas square tables are compact and can be tucked neatly into a corner if need be. Rectangular tables are ideal for larger rooms; some styles have extra leaves to extend when needed. Many oval tables can also be extended.

CHECKLIST

ESSENTIALS
- Table
- Chairs
- Lighting
- Tablecloths, mats & runners
- Napkins

GOOD TO HAVE
- Music
- Candles
- Vases
- Candles
- Corkscrew

DINING CHAIRS

The style of your chairs should reflect the tone you want to set for your table. High backed and firmly upholstered chairs convey a formal 'dinner party' feeling while mix-and-match bistro chairs are relaxed enough to be used at any time of the day.

The styles don't all have to match either, so long as your look is deliberate. Over time, you could build up a nice group of second-hand timber chairs or even paint each a different colour. They don't all have to match the table exactly either, but they should suggest a similar 'feel', that is relaxed and casual or smart and formal.

Armless chairs are the traditional choice but if room allows, carver chairs with arms offer relaxed and comfortable seating.

If space is tight, spare chairs may be kept in a hall or bedroom when not in use or you may prefer fold-away styles. For a neat alternative to traditional seating, benches can also be tucked under the table when not in use or double up as coffee tables.

Chair comfort is equally as important as shape. Straight, rigid backs are uncomfortable over a long meal so look for designs which have a gentle sway to support the lower spine. The shape of the legs should be in keeping with the style of the table.

The seat should be generous in length and the height should be suitable for your table. Padded, upholstered chairs offer the most comfort, but a removable pad can also be added to a wooden or metal seat. Removable, washable slip covers protect upholstery and can be changed seasonally to give your room an easy new look.

> **TIP** : *Adhesive felt pads on dining chair legs will protect hard floors from scuffing.*

LIGHTING

A central dining table will need a variety of lighting levels to suit the various activities that go on there.

During the day, windows allow the best possible natural light so it's good to have adjustable window treatments to take full advantage of this.

At night, having direct overhead lighting, as well as a variety of other sources including lamps and candles, is best for providing atmosphere, highlights and interest.

Direct overhead room lighting should be adjustable so it can be turned up for situations requiring bright, clean light and down to create a calm, soft ambience which is so important for the mood of a meal. Pendant lights can also be installed directly over a table, either individually or in groupings, while bulbs of different wattages and types can create a range of effects.

Lighting from one central source can create dark, shadowy corners so to easily balance this, use lamps arranged evenly around the room. Floor standing, as well as table lamps add variety and new shades can be added seasonally to update their look.

Use the opportunity to add extra glow to a room by using candles; arrange them in groups clustered down the centre of your table for a dramatic effect.

TABLE DRESSING

Though not essential, any table looks and feels much better when made up for a meal with either a cloth, runners or mats. Simple fabrics and materials always have fresh appeal and will mix and match easily with brighter colours and decorations to suit the occasion.

TABLECLOTHS

A tablecloth needs to be no more than a simple length of fabric and can dress the dullest and most uninspiring table for any meal or occasion.

The best quality cloths and napkins are made from pure linen or cotton because both are such beautiful and durable fabrics. They will withstand years of heavy laundering and always look good, so it's worth having a few in your collection.

Linen cloths with minimal detailing always look classically elegant and are among my favourites for the table. Linen is a natural fibre and really does become better with age. The higher quality Irish and Belgian types are woven using silky flax fibres which produce a soft, absorbent and long-lasting cloth, perfectly suitable for tablecloths, napkins or tea towels.

Quality linen is smooth and even and has no coarse knots. Its superior weave and fibre give it extra body and durability, however being natural it will crush easily. For a casual setting I don't mind a few wrinkles and think the creases add a soft, relaxed charm to the table. If you insist on smooth linen however, remove the washed cloth from the clothes line while it's still damp and iron on the hottest setting.

Linen has a neutral colour which is soft and easy on the eye but it can also be purchased bleached white or dyed.

Cotton is a popular choice for napery because it is relatively well priced, easy to care for and long lasting. There are many qualities available, however one of the best and most well known is Egyptian cotton.

Cotton feels more substantial but is generally prone to more shrinkage than linen and also crushes easily. Sometimes a synthetic fibre is added to the weave for ease of care. Over time, natural cotton becomes significantly softer and in my opinion better.

> **TIP** : *Plain white cotton cloths can be gently bleached to remove stains.*

SIZE OF TABLECLOTH   The size of tablecloth and length of the drape will affect how casual or formal the table will look.

- *Casual* settings have at least 20cm drop on all sides.
- *Elegant* settings have at least 60cm drop on all sides.
- *Theatrical* settings can have a cloth which reaches all the way to the floor and beyond. This is called 'puddling'.

TABLE RUNNERS

Used instead of a cloth, table runners can add casual elegance to a table setting. Place them across the table under the plates or down the centre under the serving dishes.

PLACE MATS

Mats are a simple and effective way to add colour and style to any plain table setting. I like to have a few sets in various fabrics and textures for different occasions. Buy place mats with generous proportions so they can be seen under the largest of dinner plates. As well as being decorative, thicker mats can also help to protect the table surface from hot plates.

NAPKINS

Pure cotton or linen napkins are soft, absorbent and far nicer to use than synthetic fabrics. And in my house, bigger is always better – they should cover your entire lap.

White napkins are essential for simple elegance while coloured or stylised designs can be used for special occasions or as accents. Fold napkins simply for the most stylish setting and launder them well to prevent staining. Natural cotton and linen napkins will be easier to iron while still damp.

MUSIC

For dinner parties, music should be light in tone and have an even tempo. The volume should be adjusted so it is loud enough to be heard, without competing with your guests' conversation. Compiling a continuous play list will save you having to restart the music throughout the meal.

CANDLES

Inferior candles billow black smoke so buy good quality, clean-burning types for the dinner table. Pillar candles can be clustered in groups and are more stable than tapered styles; always place candles on a stand or plate to prevent melted wax running onto the cloth. Scented candles should never be used in the dining area as perfume will compete with the enjoyment of the meal.

> **TIP** : *To remove candle wax from a tablecloth, pick away the excess wax, then place brown paper or paper towel over the area. Iron the paper on a medium setting to melt the wax. Replace the paper as often as needed. Launder as usual.*

VASES

Tall vases of flowers should be removed from the table prior to eating so as not to restrict conversation. During the meal, an alternative is an arrangement or grouping that is low and wide. I find the most useful vases are shallow glass bowls, simply styled, in various shapes and sizes.

> **TIP** : *Carefully select flowers for the table so their perfume won't overpower the meal and spoil its taste.*

HOW TO SET A TABLE
GLASSES

- Set each place with all of the glasses that will be used during the meal.
- The water glass is set to the right of the plate, just over the top of the knife.
- Wine glasses should sit to the right of the water glasses in the order they will be used, usually white then red.

CHINA

- Place the side or bread plate to the left hand side of the dining setting.
- A first-course soup bowl or salad plate can be set directly on top of a large dinner plate which is sometimes referred to as a charger. This is purely decorative and not essential.
- If you use them, chargers should be cleared along with the first course bowl or plate.
- The main meal should be delivered to the table on dinner plates once it is ready.

CUTLERY

- Set the knives and forks on the table in the order they will be used, from the outside in.
- The fork for the first course is set to the outside left of the setting, and to the left of the main meal fork.
- The knife for the first course is set to the outside right.
- The main meal fork is set closest to the dinner plate on the left side.
- The main meal knife is set closest to the right side.
- Any spoons needed before dessert, like soup spoons, should be placed to the outside right of the knives.

DESSERT TABLE SETTING

- When dessert is served, all empty wineglasses, plates, sauces, serving dishes and salt and pepper pots should be cleared away from the table.
- Dessert cutlery can either be set above the dinner plate at the initial table setting, or it can arrive on a tray at dessert time, along with dessert wine glasses.
- Water glasses should remain on the table throughout the meal, as should a jug of water.
- You may want to serve coffee or tea along with the dessert, in which case bring out the cups and saucers then. Otherwise, set out the coffee or tea cups and saucers after the dessert dishes have been cleared away.

Dinnerware

Purism is not something I usually subscribe to but I
do enjoy serving delicious food in a simple rather than
fussy style. Dinnerware should enhance the food not
distract from it because, after all, which is the real star
of the show — the meal or the table?

SHOPPING FOR DINNERWARE

For serving food, I prefer to keep things simple. Not a big fan of over-ornate settings, I like to focus instead on good food and company. For me, an essential is a clean table with comfortable seating – and a cloth is always lovely.

I have no fast and firm rules when it comes to what should go with what. Of course there are guidelines I like to follow – especially when it comes to more formal settings – but I never follow them slavishly.

What I suggest for dining and serving are items which are easy to come by and easy to replace if needed – in other words, a sensible selection of things that can serve double duty. Go for simple styling and avoid highly coloured or patterned designs which can distract from the food and date quickly. Sets may not always be the best option as they can contain items you will rarely use. My advice is to buy plates, cups and bowls individually where possible to allow greater choice plus the ability to replace easily if anything breaks.

> **TIP** : *It's easy to change the look of an otherwise plain dinner setting by adding a few unusually shaped or coloured 'accent' pieces to suit the occasion.*

CHECKLIST

ESSENTIALS
- Dinner plates
- Side plates
- Pasta bowls
- Dessert bowls
- Cups & saucers
- Mugs
- Egg cups
- Large salad bowl
- Serving platters
- Vegetable serving dishes
- Casserole dish with lid
- Sauce jug
- Milk jug
- Teapot

GOOD TO HAVE
- Individual salad plates & bowls
- Soup bowls
- Rice & noodle bowls
- Mustard & pickle dishes
- Butter dishes
- Soup tureen with lid
- Large salad dish
- Chargers (large, decorative dinner plates)

CASUAL AND FORMAL DINNERWARE

Depending on how you like to cook, eat and entertain, your table can be set either in a casual or formal manner. Although casual will do for most days, being prepared for both makes good sense. Eating more formally can really add to the overall enjoyment of the food you have prepared, to say nothing of imparting a real sense of occasion.

CASUAL DINING   For a casual place setting you will need:

- dinner plate
- side plate (suitable for bread, salad or dessert)
- medium bowl (suitable for pasta, salad, cereal, soup, stir-fry or dessert)
- tea or coffee cup and saucer or mug

FORMAL DINING   For a formal place setting you will need:

- charger (large plate under dinner plate)
- dinner plate
- salad plate
- side plate
- soup bowl
- dessert bowl
- tea or coffee cup and saucer

TYPES OF DINNERWARE

Dinnerware is commonly made from porcelain, bone china, stoneware or earthenware. As a general rule of thumb, regardless of material, white or ivory plates and bowls are considered classic and should form the base of your range.

PORCELAIN

The appearance, price and durability of porcelain make it one of the top-selling forms of dinnerware in the world. Porcelain does, however, vary in terms of quality and thickness, so I would suggest shopping around for the known brands if you want the best.

High quality porcelain feels light and smooth and is equal in strength to bone china. It can be used every day and has a hard non-porous surface which resists staining and scuffing. These days, most types can be placed safely in the oven, microwave and dishwasher – but it's always best to check first.

BONE CHINA

Bone china is a pure and fine textured form of porcelain that is considered to be one of the best qualities of dinnerware you can buy. Bone ash is added to make the china strong, translucent and very white and although it looks and feels both thin and fragile, it is actually incredibly strong as well as chip and scratch resistant.

Most pieces can be used every day in the oven, microwave and dishwasher, with the exception of metal-rimmed styles.

STONEWARE

Stoneware is a heavier and more opaque type of dinnerware than porcelain or bone china. If you prefer pieces with a little more thickness and weight, you should look for stoneware. Naturally it has a grey colour and is slightly textured but it's commonly glazed in a wide range of colours and finishes.

Often used for baking dishes and casseroles, stoneware is durable for everyday use; it is generally safe to go in the oven, microwave and dishwasher.

EARTHENWARE

Heavier and thicker than porcelain and bone china, earthenware is easier to chip and break. Made from grey or red-brown clay and ground stone, it needs to be glazed to hold liquids.

Rustic-styled dinnerware is often made of earthenware and care should be taken when placing these items in hot ovens. Gentle hand-washing is strongly recommended.

> **TIP** : *In higher quality dinnerware, the maker's mark will often be stamped on the underside, along with oven and dishwasher recommendations.*

Cutlery

Fashions come and go so if you want
cutlery with 'timeless' appeal,
it's best to avoid over-styled designs.
I like to keep things simple and choose
clean, classic lines without too much
detailing and opt for pieces that have
a good weight but are still easy to
hold. Materials and prices do vary
considerably but for my money,
a quality set of solid stainless steel
is difficult to beat.

ESSENTIALS

Teaspoons

Dinner forks

Dinner knives

Dessert spoons

GOOD TO HAVE

Steak knives

Soup spoons

Salad or entrée forks

Salad or entrée knives

Dessert forks

Dessert knives

Large serving spoons & forks

Butter knives

Cheese knives

Paté knives

Cake forks & server

Fish forks & knives

SHOPPING FOR CUTLERY

The price you will pay for new cutlery is usually related to brand as well as how the pieces are made and from what. Most shops sell pieces individually so it's easy to buy or replace exactly what you need either all at once or as money allows.

If your budget allows, you may like to consider buying extra settings – especially if you like to throw big dinner parties. It's a real bore having to rinse cutlery between courses, so do make sure your drawers are stocked with enough to cater for all.

When considering how many pieces to buy, it can be easier to think about what you need in terms of place settings and how many people you would generally cook for. My ideal is enough settings for at least four couples with two spare, that is, ten individual pieces of each item.

When buying new cutlery, try to coordinate the style to that of your plates, bowls and glassware. So if what you already have is fairly plain, go for simple styles. If your dinnerware reflects a certain period or trend, then cutlery that's a little more ornate may be suitable. And while it's perfectly acceptable to mix styles together, your overall setting should look deliberate, and definitely not accidental.

CASUAL AND FORMAL CUTLERY SETTINGS

While most of us could easily get by each day with just a fork, spoon and knife, formal dining tends to involve a bit more rummaging in the cutlery drawer.

CASUAL CUTLERY   For casual dining you will need:

- dinner fork
- dinner knife
- dessert spoon

FORMAL CUTLERY   For formal dining you will need:

- salad or entrée fork
- salad or entrée knife
- dinner fork
- dinner knife
- dessert spoon
- tea or coffee spoons

TYPES OF CUTLERY

The range of cutlery available these days can be a little overwhelming. Your final choice may be a matter of how easy – or hard – the pieces will be to care for.

STAINLESS STEEL

Ferret around in most people's kitchen drawers these days and you tend to find their knives and forks are made from stainless steel. That's because it's well priced, looks good and is easy to care for.

The best stainless steel is graded – turn the handle over to see an imprint of 18/8 or 18/10. There is very little difference between the two and either will be fine for everyday use.

Dishwashers are generally considered safe for most common brands of stainless steel but it's a good idea to pre-rinse first, especially if you leave items to sit while waiting for a full load.

SILVER-PLATED CUTLERY

Having to polish silverware on a regular basis is just too time-consuming for most of us but if you are so inclined, you might like to consider a set of silver-plated pieces.

The highest quality plated cutlery is known as EPNS (electro-plated nickel silver) and often you will see these letters stamped somewhere on the piece along with various other markings which can indicate the manufacturer and the country of origin.

STERLING SILVER CUTLERY

Because pure silver is too soft to be practical for use in silverware, small amounts of copper are added for strength, and this is known as sterling silver.

Sterling silver is generally more expensive than silver plate because it made up of over 90% actual silver. Like silver plate, sterling silver should be hand washed only and polished on a regular basis.

> **TIP** : *Cutlery with plastic, bone, ivory and pewter handles is often a little harder to care for. It usually needs to be washed by hand.*

Glassware

A generous glass filled to the brim with ice cold
water will quench the driest of thirsts and while
cooking, what could be better than drinking wine
from a bowl perfectly adequate to accommodate
a small gold fish?

CHECKLIST

ESSENTIALS

- Tumblers
- Tall water glasses
- White wine glasses
- Red wine glasses
- Water jug

GOOD TO HAVE

- Hi-ball glasses
  (for pre-dinner drinks)
- Water glasses
  (goblets with stem)
- Champagne flutes
- Whiskey glasses
- Brandy glasses
- Martini glasses
- Cocktail glasses
- Beer glasses
- Shot glasses
- Decanter

CHOOSING GLASSWARE

I consider new glassware in terms of not only what is affordable, but also what is enjoyable to use every day as well as for special occasions. The types and styles you choose need to be in keeping with your other tableware as well as your family's needs, so as to avoid tears if and when accidents occur.

An everyday set as well a range of higher quality glasses for special occasions is the ideal. For every day, possibly the most affordable and practical is machine-made glass, while for really special occasions the best you can buy is lead crystal.

A glass cupboard should be filled with a compact range of sizes suitable for both everyday use and special occasions. Simply styled, clear glasses always look good and have timeless appeal. The price you pay will depend on brand, what the glass is produced from and how it was made.

Water, soft drink and spirits generally require a flat-based, straight-sided tumbler or glass while wines can be served in glasses with or without stems.

TIP : The signs of a good glass are clarity, reasonable weight, and a thin, even rim which is comfortable to drink from. Always hold a glass before you buy.

SHOPPING FOR GLASSWARE

A sparkling array of glassware in a store can send your mind into confusion. Considering the care various types of glasses will require – and of course your budget – may make the decision making a little easier. As well, it is important to establish what sorts of beverages you usually drink and the styles of glasses you prefer.

Take the numbers you will need into account too. My ideal is enough settings for at least four couples with two spare – that is, ten individual pieces of each style. It's also worth adding an extra set of everyday small tumblers for young children and taller ones for teens.

Classically shaped, clear glassware never goes out of fashion and handled with care, will always look good. Generally I tend to avoid fussy shapes, highly patterned, foiled and coloured glassware as it's often difficult to replace if damaged. Simple styling is elegant and will coordinate with most dinnerware and cutlery styles.

The price you pay for new glassware will depend on brand, what the glass is made from and how it was made. Once considered a luxury item due to labour-intensive manufacturing, glassware is now one of the most affordable things you can buy for the home. Most glassware you will see in department stores has been machine made and is perfectly acceptable for even the most stylish table. You can of course pay more for the look and feel of hand-blown glass, which often has less uniformity, no seams and more character than machine-made glass.

CRYSTAL GLASS

Quality crystal is often chosen for its superior feel, clarity and sparkle, usually due to the high lead oxide content. The best quality contains around 24% or more lead oxide and any crystal that is hand cut usually contains this amount or more, otherwise the crystal would be too brittle to cut or engrave.

Lead crystal is considered safe to drink from but lead free crystal may also be purchased.

CARING FOR GLASS AND STEMWARE

Avoid bumping glasses together when carrying or washing up and always hand wash quality pieces separately. Handle wine glasses individually by the stem and never clutch them in a bouquet with the bowls clinking together.

Quality glassware or crystal should be washed by hand as the heat and detergent in a dishwasher can dull, scratch and cloud the surface. Scouring pads or harsh abrasives should also be avoided.

When washing glasses by hand, rinse in clean, warm water and dry with a soft lint-free cloth. Avoid twisting the bowl in the opposite direction to the stem as this can cause damage, and don't pour icy liquids into warm glasses. Because the rims are the most fragile part of the glass, never place upside down on a draining board or when storing.

> **TIP** : *To clean glass vases or decanters half-fill them with warm water, then add two tablespoons of vinegar or ammonia and a small amount of uncooked rice. Swirl for a few minutes to remove any residue inside, then rinse and dry.*

relax

A living or lounge room is often the communal area of the home and as such has to serve in a variety of ways. For times when we want to relax, curl up and nap, or quietly read it should be soothing and comfortable. But this busy room also needs to quickly adapt to feel lively and fresh when entertaining. It also should be able to comfortably seat everyone in the household as well as friends who may drop by.

Furnishings & lighting

As the main area for television viewing, home theatre and games, a lounge area also accommodates a good deal of equipment and wiring, so careful consideration needs to be given to storage as well as room layout. Essential furnishings for this room are a long-term investment, so take time to carefully consider comfort and durability. Choose styles and fabrics for their timeless appeal.

THE SOFA

How you want a sofa to look and feel as well as how you intend to use it will determine what kind of shape, colour and size you need to buy. A sofa should be soft and inviting yet supportive and well cushioned. It should have good shape, generous seating and reflect the style of the room.

SHOPPING FOR A SOFA

For a sofa long enough to fully stretch out on you should look for something low and relatively deep. This style can also help to open up a small room as the low back can make the walls seem taller and the ceiling higher.

A higher backed sofa with concealed legs will look solid and heavy and appear to take up more space than those with visible legs. To give the illusion of space in the room, select styles where the legs are visible. Neutral coloured and unfussy fabrics are the best choice for long-term style and the ability to easily accessorise for new looks. For a sofa which will last many years, select a kiln-dried hardwood frame and coil inner springs. The cushioning and padding should be chosen to suit your comfort needs.

CHECKLIST

ESSENTIALS
- Sofa
- Armchair
- Coffee table
- Window treatments

GOOD TO HAVE
- Ottoman or footstool
- Console tables
- Floor lamps & table lamps
- Occasional tables
- Scatter cushions
- Rugs & throws

POPULAR SOFA STYLES *Sectional or modular* sofas offer modern styling and usually consist of a group of individual chair sections. These can often be purchased separately to suit the size and shape of your room. A basic grouping can have end chairs with either a left or right arm as well as middle sections (no arms either side) and a corner section if needed.

Classic sofas have a style which is considered timeless. They are often oversized and skirted with curved, roll arms and turned legs. There are modern variations to this look, however it still remains a true favourite for both casual and formal settings.

Tailored sofas offer a neat style with trim shaping and firm seating. The chair backs are often tight or buttoned while the seat cushioning is bench or slim style.

SOFA STRUCTURE All upholstered furniture is generally assembled the same way using a frame, possibly springs, padding and fabric.

The frame is what makes your sofa strong and durable. It should be secured with glue, dowel and screws as opposed to nail gun pinning. Kiln dried hardwood and beech are considered among the best whereas softwood frames generally don't keep their shape.

Care should be taken not to situate sofas directly near air vents or radiators where sudden temperature changes can cause the frame to warp permanently.

SPRINGS AND FILL The best sofas have springs in both the seat and the back however most coil sofas are sprung in the seat only. Heavy-gauge steel springs will provide support and good shape over many years of use whereas inferior sofas will often sag. These usually have nylon webbing to support the cushions instead of strong coil springs. Don't be shy about asking questions – and getting answers – about the types of springs and filling in the sofas you are considering. It's worth taking your time over such a major buying decision.

SOFA CUSHIONS The most expensive fillings for cushions are goose feathers and duck down and while they are lovely and soft, they do flatten and need puffing back into shape on a regular basis. If you do decide on feather and down-filled cushions, make sure they are encased in down-proof ticking.

A polyester fibre, feather and down mix is a good choice for sofa cushions as it will flatten less and is more manageable than pure feather and down. Regardless of their content, regular plumping of cushions will help to maintain their shape and keep them looking good. The best way to plump cushions is to punch them from all sides and drop them onto a clean floor. If possible, sofa cushions should be rotated weekly to provide even wear and guard against fading.

FABRIC AND COVERS When choosing a new sofa fabric, I always recommend avoiding highly patterned or bright colours and favour classic, neutral tonings with an interesting texture for style and longevity. Colour and interest can always be added using extra scatter cushions and throws which can be changed as often as the season – or your mood – dictates.

Most sofas are sold either fully upholstered for a tailored look or with removable covers which are a practical option and provide casual style. Some sofas are sold upholstered only in calico and you select the final covering fabric. As a guide, to cover an average two-seat sofa, you will need around 12m of fabric. For a three-seater you will require around 15m.

Linen union, closely woven cotton drill, chintz, faux suede and soft leather are all good fabric choices for sofas and can generally be pre-treated with a stain resistant coating.

Caring for the sofa fabric will help it to last so vacuum often, especially into the creases as dust and dirt can make the fabric appear dull and will accelerate the wear of the fibres. Order washable arm caps at the time of purchase.

Removable chair covers should be laundered and allowed to dry naturally away from direct sunlight and heat. Fit the covers while the fabric is still slightly damp.

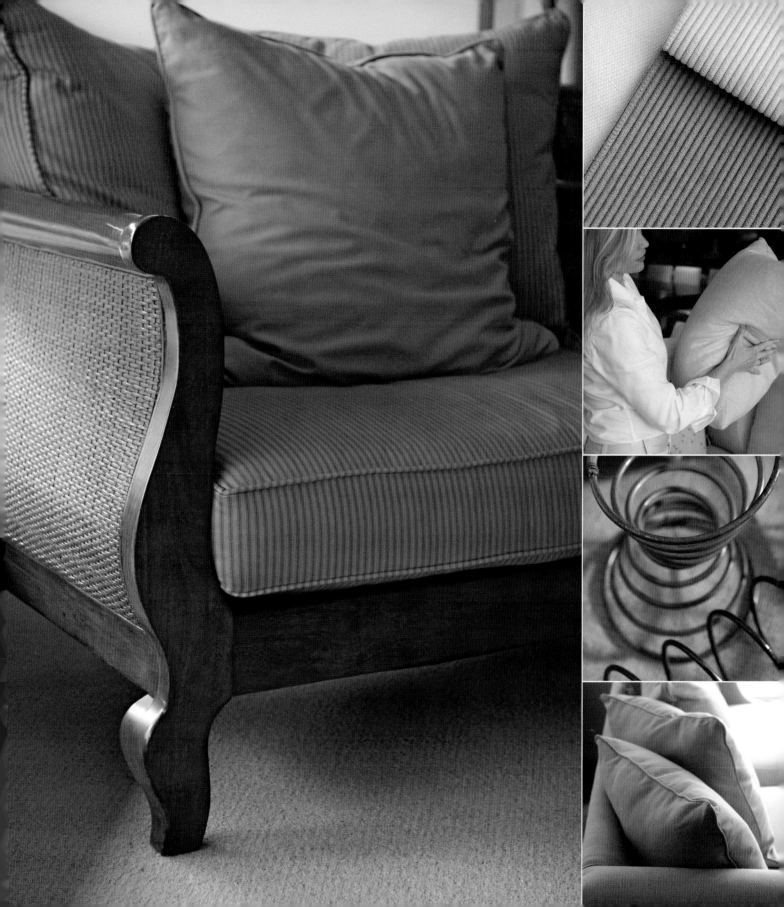

ARMCHAIRS

I like a separate armchair for solo television viewing or reading and use a footstool for a little extra comfort. Some prefer however to do away with armchairs altogether and simply use a pair of sofas instead. Either way, you should never feel compelled to select furniture which is all matching. In fact with confidence you can add far more interest to a room if things are a little mixed.

Traditional armchairs are reasonably high backed but I prefer something with a more relaxed style and deeper seat.

OTTOMANS OR FOOTSTOOLS

These offer comfort as well as extra seating and come in a wide range of sizes and styles ranging from benches to cubes. Firm cushioned styles can also double as a coffee or occasional table, provided drinks are set down on a tray.

> **TIP** : *Don't get stuck in a rut with the way you place furniture. Move it around for fresh new looks.*

COFFEE TABLE

A generous coffee table creates a real focal point in a room so don't be afraid to scale it up. Square or round are my favourite shapes but I will often compromise and use the unexpected as a table.

As well as being for practical purposes, a coffee table provides a broad surface on which to create 'table scapes', which is basically a term for groupings of favourite objects arranged together in pride of place. Unusual displays initiate conversation and add personal style to a room.

CONSOLE TABLES

A console (or sofa) table is long and narrow and can be used directly behind the sofa to place lamps, vases and magazines on. Usually measuring only around 30cm deep, and running the full length of the sofa, most rooms can accommodate – and certainly benefit from – a console.

OCCASIONAL TABLES

Generously proportioned side tables allow extra surfaces for lamps, drinks, framed photographs and small artworks, treasured mementoes and accessories.

LIGHTING

Overhead lighting should be controllable using dimmer switches and also be supplemented with a variety of lamps and candles to create a relaxing atmosphere. For those who require brighter lighting for reading and close work, consider spotlights or standard lamps.

WINDOW TREATMENTS

Window treatments in lounge areas may be chosen according to the style of the room as well as for practicality. With most lounge areas now being used as media rooms, full darkening is required for daytime movie and game viewing. Therefore, you want something that will allow the light in or block it out as needed.

Curtaining with black-out backing is an option, as are shutters and blinds. These may however allow light to filter through the blades as well as around the edges. A combination of the two can also be attractive.

> **TIP** : *The street frontage of the house should always be considered when selecting window treatments. A uniformity of style will look more consistent and appealing.*

Drapes, curtains or fabric blinds don't have to be just practical – think of them as adding yet another layer of interest and softness to a room.

Curtains can be expensive but you can save by hanging a rod above the window with a drape on either side simply for a decorative effect. For privacy, use a less expensive sheer curtaining or venetian blind to cover the window.

Sheer curtain and blind fabrics like cotton, linen and voile will diffuse sunlight during the day. They will also screen the cold look of black windows at night. For heavier weight curtaining, consider using backed cotton, linen or silk.

SCATTER CUSHIONS

I admit to having rather an obsession with scatter cushions quite simply because they can completely transform a sofa in terms of both style and comfort with minimum effort and very little cost. Always make sure you have plenty and don't be afraid to mix and match tones and fabrics for added texture, layering and interest. Polyester fill cushions are very affordable and do retain their shape while feather and down are often softer, more expensive and will need puffing back into shape after use.

In summer, choose a mixture of lightweight shimmery fabrics in fresh colours and in winter richer, plush weaves in deep tones will certainly help warm things up.

For those who love to lie on the floor, a pair of large cushions will be comfortable to rest your head on or perch against. For added durability, choose heavyweight fabric such as denim or linen.

THROWS

Draped over chairs, throws are not only incredibly stylish but are very inviting for cozy comfort on cooler days and nights. Useful for adding extra interest and layering to your design scheme, throws should be rotated between seasons and the thickness, colour and weave changed to suit the prevailing temperatures. Thick, soft wool is perfect for wintry weather whereas silk, cotton or linen add a light layer which breathes during cooler, less balmy summer evenings. Choose colours to either complement or contrast with a room's main colour.

RUGS

Regardless of what type of flooring you have, a rug or some carpeting is essential for children and adults alike who enjoy the floor for games, reading or watching TV.

A rug can bring a welcome splash of colour or warmth to a large area of the room and may be used as a main feature or simply to provide subtle and textural layering. There are many sorts of rugs to choose from. You may prefer to save up and invest in a few 'good' rugs like the exquisite, hand-knotted ones which have a high number of threads per square inch. Less costly but still beautiful options are kelims and dhurries. And there are plenty of even more affordable rugs widely available these days, in a wide range of colours, styles, sizes and shapes. Some are so low cost that it's an easy matter to replace them as they wear.

Rugs should be soft, easy to vacuum and clean, and the pile length should be suitable for the traffic it will receive, including children or pets. A rug should be generous enough in proportion to cover all of the main area of a room, say between the sofa and other furniture – and it's fine if your rug is so large that it sneaks under the sofa. A coffee or dining table can be placed on the rug if need be.

In some rooms, a sisal or jute rug may be more suitable. There are plenty to choose from. You may prefer wall-to-wall floor covering – but even so, a rug can still add interest and 'life' to a room.

> **TIP** : *Rugs may be slippery underfoot on floorboards or tiled flooring. Non-slip under-matting will solve the problem.*

Storage & accessories

Keeping up with the latest technology can be enough of a challenge, let alone finding practical, good-looking ways of accommodating all your electronic equipment.

Being one of the busiest areas of the home, the lounge room does have the tendency to become the 'dumping ground' for all sorts of clutter. As well as being the hub of the home for relaxing and watching television, this room is also the most commonly used for entertaining.

In order to have a space that serves the needs of all who live in the home, finding effective storage solutions is crucial. Not only will this help keep the clutter under control and the room looking good, but at a moment's notice it can be tidied, dusted and vacuumed with absolute ease.

Housing all things electronic as well as items like toys, books, newspapers and magazines can be achieved in smart yet affordable ways — it's simply a matter of organising a system that works. Clever storage is discreet while still being practical, accessible, flexible to your household's changing needs, and easy to clean and maintain. You can have storage shelves built-in, but although this is a streamlined solution, it tends to be expensive. Put your imagination to work and come up with viable alternatives.

TIP : Paint mismatching baskets, boxes and small furniture items in the same colour range for neat, smart-looking storage coordinates.

CHECKLIST

ESSENTIALS
- Television & electronic equipment storage
- Stereo & speaker stands
- Magazine, newspaper & book storage

GOOD TO HAVE
- Compact disc & DVD storage
- Vases
- Art pieces
- Framed prints & photographs
- Personal collections & displays

TELEVISION & ELECTRONIC EQUIPMENT

Electronic equipment is ever changing, in particular televisions. Not only are they becoming flatter, but also wider and taller. The choice now exists for them to be neatly wall mounted, floor standing or placed on a low bench rather than being housed in a more traditional cabinet.

A low console is the perfect style of furniture for attractively storing all kinds of audio-visual equipment and can be selected to suit to the style of other furniture in the room. It is also terrific for wide, flat-screened televisions and often will include a shelf underneath for DVD players, games and other entertainment paraphernalia.

Smaller, bulky televisions look much better when housed in cabinets. Older sets and assorted electrical boxes and wires can be ugly, so a cabinet with closing doors is a great way to hide the clutter when not in use.

If new storage furniture is beyond your current budget, or if you prefer something with a little more history and character, have a search around your local second-hand furniture stores as many of the older styles of console tables and buffets can be easily adapted to suit modern electrical equipment.

COMPACT DISC AND DVD STORAGE

Discs can be stored out of sight by stacking into cabinet drawers. Alternatively, store them in disc boxes and cases in colours and styles that coordinate with your design scheme. Wall shelves free up floor space while still allowing easy access and floor standing storage will hold a large collection.

MAGAZINES, NEWSPAPERS AND BOOKS

A coffee table with a sturdy shelf directly underneath is ideal for storing magazines and books – and keeps the table top clear. Baskets are a neat solution for newspapers, magazines, games and toys; ones with lids can be stacked. Bookcases can look untidy in a main living area; try to select styles with doors to conceal the mess and save time dusting.

VASES

Vases reserved especially for the lounge area encourage fresh ideas for display. For dynamic impact, buy either one very large vase or several smaller vases in the same – or similar – colour, shape and style.

Vases don't always need to be filled with large bunches of flowers. Try displaying a single stem, group of twigs or selection of green foliage from the garden. Glass vases are especially suited for grouping and displaying small things you love to collect – some of my favourites are match boxes, shells, feathers and photographs.

ART PIECES, PRINTS AND PHOTOGRAPHS

One of my favourite ways to liven up a room is to hang pictures. These can either be original paintings or framed prints or photographs. If funds are short, inject a little colour and style with art you create yourself. Art shops sell stretched canvas on frames in a range of sizes. A length of fabulous fabric stapled over a timber frame can look stunning and takes only minutes to do.

Scale is very important and where possible, I tend to hang one or two very large pictures for impact or group smaller pictures together on the same wall for maximum appeal. Frames can be arranged according to their colour or type or the pictures united by a similar colour, subject or theme.

PERSONAL COLLECTIONS AND DISPLAYS

Nothing makes you feel more at home than when you are surrounded by your favourite things – but don't let collections get out of hand. If you are a real hoarder, consider glass cabinets or modular shelving with inbuilt lighting to show off your pieces. If space is at a premium, pack away some of your collection and rotate selected items seasonally.

To display items to their best advantage, arrange them in small groups according to a theme. Look for new ways to show off a collection to keep the room from looking tired.

bathe

In the bathroom, my secret for classic appeal is to keep things simply styled and to never introduce bold colours into anything that can't be changed quickly and easily. Colour, interest, brightness and pattern can be added using inexpensive accessories. What could be simpler than changing a few towels and trinkets to have a completely new look as often as the mood takes you?

Design & furnishings

No longer is the bathroom seen as merely a practical and clinical space.
It's now being furnished as a seductive area for relaxation and pampering.

CHECKLIST

ESSENTIALS
Waterproof walls & flooring
Sink
Shower & bath
Taps
Lighting
Shower screen
Mirror

GOOD TO HAVE
Storage cabinet or shelves
Chair or seat
Hooks for towels & robes
Clothing hamper
Window dressing

CHOOSING BATHROOM MATERIALS

With a greater choice of materials, fixtures and fittings on the market than ever, you really do need to take great care to select bathroom basics wisely so the room not only will fulfil its multiple purposes, but also won't date too quickly.

The bathroom is one area where it can be very easy to spend ridiculous amounts of money – and what you choose can add to, or even detract from, the value of your home. My advice is to understand your needs and preferences and do your best to keep a clear head when considering colours, surface finishes, shapes and styles.

There are also practical, behind-the-scenes things to consider when decorating and furnishing a bathroom. Costs can be minimised if the plumbing doesn't have to be relocated. Make sure the hot water tank will service the whole family's needs. There is nothing worse than running out of hot water halfway through a shower or having it run cold when another tap is turned on. And of course all fittings and fixtures must be impervious to water and easy to keep hygienically clean.

> **TIP** : *Light-coloured walls and floors will make a bathroom seem larger, so to give the illusion of space try using colours from the natural palette.*

WALLS AND FLOORING

Hygiene is paramount in the bathroom, so tiling the floor and cladding the walls is a practical choice. Glazed tiles and glass not only look good but will stand up to harsh cleaning products and can be wiped down easily. Porous surfaces like natural or composite stone will need to be sealed for durability. Always consider safety as many bathroom materials are slippery and hazardous when wet.

TILES

Tiles vary significantly in terms of material, size and price. They can be laid across the entire floor area and either partially or fully up the walls. Tiles extended up to the ceiling can give the illusion of extra height and make the bathroom appear larger.

Ceramic tiles are one of the most low maintenance and affordable options with non-porous types such as glazed, quarry, and porcelain never needing to be sealed or polished. Available in various finishes, sizes and thicknesses, these tiles are especially suited for either floor and/or wall applications.

Shade variation can cause tile colour to vary from batch to batch, so if you are buying in reasonable quantities make sure that all the tiles you are being given are from the same batch. Any left-over boxes should be returned quickly as most suppliers won't accept returns on any that don't match what they are currently selling.

In terms of design, I recommend avoiding stylised 'fashion' tiles or bright colours and motifs as they can quickly date a bathroom. Size is important here, and for my money I prefer a larger format tile. Mosaic and mini tiles are high fashion and while they do look fabulous will tend to date more quickly. If using larger tiles, consider introducing contemporary interest with up-to-the-minute towels and accessories such as a couple of vases or pieces of art.

For a seamless, coordinated look, grout should be selected in a shade similar to the body of the tiles. Apply grout sealer to keep it looking fresh.

STANDARD TILE SIZES

- 10 x 10cm
- 20 x 10cm
- 20 x 20cm
- 30 x 30cm
- 30 x 60cm
- 40 x 40cm
- 60 x 60cm

TIP : *Mirrors are a great way to add depth, width and length to a small bathroom. They can also help to distribute light throughout the room.*

Glass tiles and splashbacks are a beautiful but expensive option. Full sheets of glass can be used to line the shower recess or main bathroom walls and can be textured, sandblasted or coloured. Full sheets can also be custom made to cover a large area without joins.

Natural stone and marble can look stunning but will need regular sealing and maintenance to prevent staining and absorption. Some types can also be extremely slippery.

Polished concrete and terrazzo are good choices for bathroom areas for an industrial or warehouse feel. Slabs can be poured on site or laid in tile form. In cooler climates, you may wish to consider under-floor heating as tiled or concrete surfaces can be cold underfoot.

PAINT

Bathrooms are particularly damp, humid areas and generally require mould inhibitor to be added to ceiling and wall paints to minimise spores. Many of the larger paint manufacturers make paints which are specifically suited to these areas; these can be tinted to a variety of colours. Otherwise regular paints may be used with the addition of an anti-fungal agent. Keep in mind that mid sheen to high gloss paint finishes are much easier to clean than matt finishes and coarse textures, while effects like pearlescent and metallics can easily be applied to provide rich, luxurious appeal.

CABINETS

A bathroom can feel so much bigger by simply allowing more of the floor area to be seen. This can be achieved by using a wall mounted or pedestal sink, wall shelves and cabinets.

Bench surfaces should be smooth, well sealed and easy to clean. Stone, composite stone, sheet metal, synthetic or laminated board are all good choices.

Cupboards and shelves made from timber need to be sealed for durability in the bathroom. While laminated particle board is an affordable and durable choice, care must be taken to ensure damaged or open edges remain dry, otherwise swelling can occur.

SINKS

Deciding on a sink can be difficult, but always consider simple styling and a practical shape. Sinks can be part of a cabinet or bench and either recessed, semi-recessed or exposed, such as a bowl. Pedestal styles will save space but they offer little in terms of storage or surfaces for accessories. Porcelain is the classic material for sinks and is non porous and easy to clean. Other options include glass, stone, composite stone, stainless steel and chrome.

Taps are available in a huge range of styles and should complement the design of the room and other accessories. Some types may require pipes to be in a different position to what is already in place, so check with your plumber to see if what you are considering is possible. Taps should be easy to clean and use.

A basin set can include the spout and two taps or a mixer tap which combines the spout and a single lever all in one. The hot and cold water in a mixer tap are combined so the temperature and flow rate can be adjusted easily with less risk of dangerous scalding.

BATHS

While I love the refreshing convenience of a shower, for the occasional home pampering treat, I do think you can't beat a hot bubble bath. Such an affordable luxury as a bath tub should always be included in your design scheme if space allows. For small children they are essential – and for grown-ups a long soak can soothe all aches and pains. A bath tub, being so large, will become the focal point of the room so shape and position are important. But even smaller bathrooms can accommodate shorter, deeper models or shower combinations.

CHOOSING A BATH   Steel and vitrious enamel baths are solid, stable and will be long lasting whereas acrylic baths may not feel as substantial, but are still very strong and affordable.

White is always a classic choice and a bath with central taps and waste will be more comfortable whichever way you face. Some baths include spa jets while corner tubs save space.

SHOWERS

Shower screens are essential for keeping the water within the confines of the showering area and can be made from either curtaining, glass or tiled wall. Screens can be custom made to be used in conjunction with a tiled floor, hob or bath edge and can be fixed or hung using hinges, brackets, frames or poles.

Framed and semi-framed shower screens are smart, relatively clean lined and more suitable for homes with children than frameless screens. Framed styles offer more stability than frameless and are usually more affordable too.

Framed glass screens are usually made from powder coated aluminium or stainless steel. For simple elegance, match the frame to the wall tiles or use a silver colour in either a satin or gloss finish. Two- or three-sided frames are suitable for larger bathrooms; a corner style is a more efficient use of space.

Frameless shower screens are expensive but their clean-lined, modern look will make a small bathroom seem bigger. Glass can be clear, sandblasted, laminated, or patterned.

Shower curtains should be as waterproof as possible and the fabric needs to be heavy in weight. This will help to stop the curtain from wrapping and clinging to your body during showering. The fabric should be washable and cleaned on a regular basis to prevent mould.

Shower heads can be either fixed to the wall or ceiling, hand held or adjustable and can be paired with many different styles of tapware.

A shower head on a rail can be moved to different heights and hand held for easy rinsing. This is my pick for its convenience for everyone in the household.

Rain showers have a large head with a wide spray pattern and produce a shower that really does feel like rain. Water saving models are available and the better qualities have optional massage heads as well as the ability to adjust the mounting height.

A single lever mixer tap can be used instead of two taps which I think is a safer option especially for children. The water temperature is mixed together rather than having to turn one tap on, then adjust with the other.

TOILETS

Toilets can be in the main bathroom area, in a separate room or concealed within an alcove. If possible, position them away from the main flow of bathroom traffic. Make sure they will be easy to clean. A covered 's' bend gives a streamlined look.

Newer models have touch-pad flushing plus dual-flush options and the cistern can be completely housed within the wall or ceiling cavity or connected directly to the mains system. On these models, the pan is usually mounted on a reinforced internal wall to carry the weight.

> **TIP** : *Towel rails are needed to dry and air towels between showering and can be as simple as a floor standing ladder. A heated towel rail is a real bonus in damp weather or if you have a big family with lots of towels to dry.*

> **TIP** : *Window dressing should be light and airy to allow steam to escape especially if that is your only method of venting. Shutters are not only cleanable but also adjustable to allow daylight and air through while still giving complete privacy. This type of window treatment means you don't have to frost the window glass.*

VENTILATION

Good ventilation is a must in all bathrooms. If you have a window, open it up on a regular basis to air the bathroom. In bathrooms without windows, an effective ceiling exhaust fan is essential.

LIGHTING

The bathroom needs to cater for all kinds of lighting requirements so it's best to have several sources. For the sink and mirror areas, I like to use halogen lights on either side of the mirror to create a flattering, balanced light to the face. These can be controlled with a dimmer switch to be bright when needed and soft and subdued for relaxing. Combination ceiling light, exhaust fan and heaters are an excellent idea, but should be supplemented with additional, separate lighting. Overall room lighting should be controllable and balanced to avoid dark areas.

STORAGE

Good storage methods in the bathroom prevent the clutter which makes a small room feel even smaller and cleaning far too difficult. There are plenty of imaginative yet neat ways to utilise every square inch of space and help keep your bathroom a haven.

- Exposed shelving or floating cabinets give the impression of more floor space.
- Drawers with compartments keep the order.
- A wheelable trolley is portable and space efficient.
- Glass jars and clear tubs keep everything in place.
- Small baskets on the bench top are perfect for pretty soaps.
- Baskets with lids can be stacked to save space.
- A seat with built-in storage serves double duty.
- A wall cabinet clears the bench and doubles as a mirror.

Towels & accessories

For the perfect bathroom, combine the practical with the more sensual,
soft fabrics and textures, as well as a few of your favourite soaps
and lotions, to create your very own private oasis.

ESSENTIALS
- Standard bath towels (3 per person)
- Hand towels (3 per sink)
- Bath mats (3 per shower or bath)
- Soaps
- Brushes

GOOD TO HAVE
- Bath sheets (large towels)
- Hair towels (optional)
- Face cloths (3 per person)
- Lotions
- Candles
- Robes

AFFORDABLE BATHROOM LUXURY

Most consider a bathroom to be purely functional – but for something far more inviting, why not have a room as comfortable and relaxing as a day spa? It really can be so simple, and whether your bathroom is new or old, start by freshening things up – give it a good spring clean.

Clear out any old lotions, medicines and threadbare towels, wipe down shelves and polish the mirror. Consider adding a shelf for extra storage as well as to make the perfect area to display accessories. An extra rail and hook are ideal for quick hanging, and if space allows a small chair or stool is great for placing clothes while bathing or for sitting to do nails.

Once that's done, you're ready to stock up on a few new bathroom essentials – and perhaps even some extra pampering treats. Start with classic, quality white towels, some softly scented soaps, a few new brushes and an array of sparkling glass jars filled to the brim with cotton buds, wipes and bath salts.

TIP : *White towels always look good and can be bleached and laundered regularly without fading. Use nappy soak to really brighten them.*

TOWELS

A towel can be coarse fibred, soft and fluffy or somewhere in between. The choice is purely personal but what does make one towel better than the next is its absorbency and resistance to fading, shrinking and distorting. When buying towels, look for a substantial feel, a long, thick pile and a good, tight weave.

SIZE AND WEIGHT   Towels come in all sorts of thicknesses and sizes; choose them to suit the individual needs of your family. Large bath sheets can be heavy and hard to manage when damp so a smaller, more manageable towel may be better. If you wash your towels regularly, or only use a clothes dryer, smaller, more lightweight towels will dry faster and use less electricity.

TYPE   Most of the towels commonly available are cotton terry looped fabric. The longer and denser the loops, the thicker and more absorbent the towel will be. The fibre type and the way it has been woven is what gives the towel its thickness and ability to absorb as well as appearance.

- *Egyptian cotton* towels are among the best you can buy. Strong and durable with a fine, lustrous finish.
- *Pima* is an excellent type of cotton which also produces quality towels. Its extra long staple length gives ultra high absorbency, strength and durability.
- *Zero twist* gives a highly absorbent, plush cotton towel which is not too heavy.
- *Double yarn* is made by spinning two yarns together to give a thick, evenly smooth towel with very little lint.
- *Upland cotton* is the cotton used commonly for towels and is available in a variety of qualities.
- *Jacquard* towels are woven with sculpted patterns into the thick cotton fabric.
- *Cotton velour* towels have a low, velvety surface which is not as absorbent as thick plush loop types.

WASHING   The majority of washing powders contain optical brightening agents which are excellent for keeping 'whites' looking white, but they will make some pastel shades look pale and faded. Use a detergent without brighteners and wash your towels separately to preserve their colour.

Fabric conditioner should be avoided when washing towels as it leaves a fine coating on the fibres which can considerably reduce their absorbency.

New towels should be washed and tumble dried before use to make them soft and fluffy.

If you prefer to line dry, don't leave your towels in the sun any longer than necessary as their colour may fade. Choose a shady part of the garden for air drying and give them a good shake when dry to restore their softness.

SHRINKING   All natural fibres like pure cotton will shrink slightly with washing but better quality towels will resist shrinking and distortion. Washing in cold water will also help prevent shrinkage.

BATH MATS

Because it's impossible to avoid splashes, drips and sprays, every bath or shower needs at least one absorbent mat or washable rug.

A bath mat will dry quickly and easily whereas a thicker floor rug may remain damp for longer and need regular airing. A cotton rug is a good choice but may need a non-slip padding or rubber backing on the reverse for stability.

BATH ROBES

Waffle-weave cotton has a textured, honeycomb weave which makes it lightweight and highly absorbent – perfect for the summer months.

Cotton terry towelling is thick, soft and absorbent. Perfectly luxurious to slip on after a shower. Make sure there's a hook to hang it on!

BATHING ACCESSORIES

Softly textured or stimulating, natural fibres can soothe or invigorate the body and are especially well suited to the humid atmosphere of the bathroom. Bristle brushes, sponges and loofahs not only make good-looking accessories but will make you feel good too.

LOOFAH   These sponges are made from the fibrous fruit of the loofah plant. Moisten to gently exfoliate the skin.

BODY BRUSH   A wide paddle brush with natural bristles can be used dry or wet to stimulate circulation, polish your skin and keep it healthy.

SPONGE   Natural sea sponges are superior to latex and should be freshened regularly by soaking in a solution of white vinegar and warm water.

PUMICE STONE   This natural volcanic stone is indispensable for smoothing rough heels and elbows.

NAIL BRUSH   A wooden-handled, soft-bristled brush is essential for both hands and feet. Nylon bristles can be too coarse and can damage cuticles.

HAIR BRUSH   A quality hair brush is essential for healthy smooth hair. Some of the best are made from natural bristles. Ask your hairdresser to recommend one suitable for you.

SOFT FURNISHINGS

A loose covered chair or stool in the bathroom is both useful and luxurious and should be included if space will allow. Fabrics that are absorbent, like towelling and linen, are a must and can be thrown in the wash as often as your bath towels.

BATHROOM DISPLAYS

Some of the simplest and most effective decorating accessories for the bathroom are things which most people store away like soaps, lotions and oils. Consider new ways to display the toiletries you use the most and purchase them according to the colour and theme of the room.

SOAPS AND CLEANSING BARS   Soaps need to be chosen carefully as many brands are made from strong, perfumed detergents which can strip and dry the skin. Pure and vegetable oil soaps as well as glycerine and cleansing bars are a better alternative. Use a soap dish to preserve the life of the bar and stack extra blocks in jars for a great display.

CANDLES   Candles create ambience and soft mood lighting while bathing. A few better quality candles will last longer, smoke less and provide rich, perfumed fragrances. Glass jars or votives prevent liquid wax from running while varying heights add a sense of drama.

> **TIP** : *Lotions, soaps and bath oils in designer bottles can often be expensive so buy refills where possible and decant them into your own containers for coordinated and cost-effective style.*

sleep

With most of us needing around seven to eight hours of sleep per night, it's no wonder half the world is grumpy. So many people just aren't getting the sleep they need and quality rest is essential to feeling and performing your best. Of course external influences as well as the temperature, noise and light levels of your bedroom can affect the quality of sleep you have but so can your bedding.

Beds & bedding

They say we spend around one third of our lives in bed which, in my opinion,
seems far too long to be uncomfortable.

ESSENTIALS

Beds & mattresses

Pillows
(2 per person)

Quilts
(for winter & summer)

Blankets
(for winter & summer)

Pillow protectors

Mattress protector

Valances or bed skirts
(depending on bed)

Sets of sheets & pillowcases
(3 sets per bed, to alternate)

Quilt covers
(3 per bed, to alternate)

GOOD TO HAVE

Throws

Cushions

Bolster or
neck support pillow

Your bed should be one of the most luxurious things you own and a place where you can fully relax to enjoy a good and restful night's sleep. A quality bed is a long-term investment – not only in terms of your health but also for your sense of well-being. So in order to get the best sleep possible, it's worth saving up and paying that little bit extra. It will be money well spent.

Because bedding tends to be quite expensive, cheaper beds may seem more appealing at the time of purchase. However buying in this way can end up being false economy. Besides generally being uncomfortable, lesser quality beds just don't last as well. Usually made with inferior materials and construction methods, they deteriorate and lose support quickly, thereby needing to be replaced more often than premium types.

For year-round comfort, the bedding you choose is as important as the bed itself. Having the correct warmth weight as well as sheet and pillow types, can greatly affect the way you sleep, so getting comfortable for each season should be a priority. Many people forget to update and supplement basic bedding items like pillows and sheets when a few simple changes and fresh additions can really make all the difference.

SHOPPING FOR A NEW BED

As a guide, a quality mattress should be replaced every 8 to 10 years, but how it feels and looks should indicate whether it's time for a change. Comfort is a personal thing, so you really need to visit a bedding showroom and actually lie on the beds on display to choose the best one for you.

When selecting a new bed, take its size, comfort, style and durability into account. Decide before you go shopping what type of bed is most appropriate for your needs – either an ensemble or slat platform bed. Make sure it is large enough to fully stretch out on. Ideally a mattress should be at least 15cm longer than the tallest person sleeping on it.

Be sure to measure your bedroom and door widths carefully to ensure there's enough room for it, and remember to purchase a mattress protector at the same time as a new bed for hygiene reasons as well as to protect the mattress.

BEDDING TERMS
- *Ensemble* is a mattress and base set; the base may be a box or box spring base.
- *Platform* is a mattress on a solid platform base.
- *Slat* is a mattress on timber, nylon or metal slats.
- *Headboard* may be part of a platform base or separate to a box base.
- *Footboard* may be part of a platform base or separate to a box base.

BED BASES

The base of the bed is as important as the mattress as it acts as a shock absorber, provides support and adds to the durability. With ensemble beds you can choose to have inner coils in the mattress as well as the base, or simply a coil mattress on a box base. Having coils in both will provide the best support and long term value. If you opt for a bed frame without a box spring base, it's important to be sure the frame itself provides adequate central support for the mattress.

MATTRESSES

People who sleep on their backs usually prefer firm mattresses, while those who sleep on their stomachs or sides prefer soft. To gauge support, check there are at least 608 coils (for a queen size bed). The more coils, the better the bed will conform to your body.

The coil wire should be thick – number 13 gauge or lower – and a mattress should be reinforced around the outer edges to provide support. The layer over the coil construction can be polyester, wool, silk or even luxurious cashmere in the more expensive models.

Quality, breathable covering fabrics like 100% cotton damask are ideal for mattress coverings. (Damask has a design or pattern woven into it and is generally made from heavier yarns to create a fabric suitable for mattresses.)

Look for a mattress with straight seams, uniform quilting and sturdy side handles.

The quilting design on the surface can change the way a mattress feels. Small and close quilting feels firm while larger quilting feels soft. An extra topper or comforter on the mattress will add softness.

Average mattress thickness can vary from around 35cm to 50cm so if you prefer to use fitted sheets, ensure they are deep enough. The supporting base should be the same width and length as the mattress.

For taller people, a size called California king, measuring 213cm is available – but it may need to be custom made.

STANDARD BED MATTRESS SIZES
- *Single* (twin)   92cm × 190cm
- *Single* (twin extra long)   92cm × 202cm
- *King single*   107cm × 202cm
- *Double* (full)   137cm × 190cm
- *Queen*   153cm × 202cm
- *King*   203cm × 202cm
- *California king mattress*   213cm × 213cm

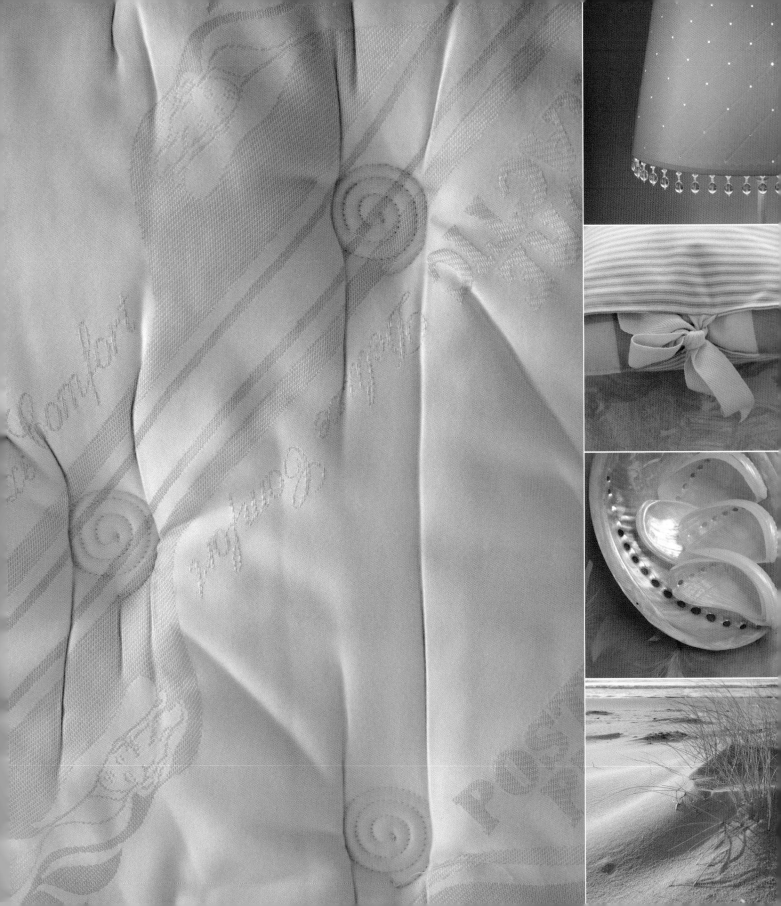

CARING FOR YOUR MATTRESS   Once you've invested in a good bed, you need to take care of it. The small investment of a mattress protector or barrier can extend the life of your mattress by keeping it fresh and clean and reducing wear on the fabric. I suggest using a mattress protector as well as or instead of a bed topper or comforter.

Rotate and flip your mattress every 4–6 weeks to encourage even wear and prevent hollows from forming. Once a month, vacuum the mattress with a soft brush attachment.

Whenever possible your mattress should be allowed to air with sheets either folded back or removed completely. Air all bedding on a dry, windy day by hanging on a clothesline away from direct sunlight.

Clean under and around your bed regularly to remove dust and lint. Having your bed on wheels allows it to be moved quickly and easily for vacuuming.

PILLOW TOPPERS OR COMFORTERS   A pillow topper is a thick, padded layer designed to increase the softness of a mattress. Some beds are sold with one 'built-in' or you may prefer to purchase a removable and cleanable one separately.

Separate toppers are available with either polyester, wool fleece, cotton or down fill and some are reversible for both summer and winter comfort. The fill should be hypoallergenic, fully washable or dry cleanable and for durability, the cotton lining should be a minimum 230 thread count. Having the sides elasticised will ensure a secure fit over the mattress; deep mattresses require a side depth of around 40cm.

PILLOWS

Choosing a pillow is one of the most important decisions to make in furnishing the bedroom. The degree of softness or firmness is a personal choice and is usually guided by how you like to fall asleep – whether on your back, stomach or side.

Allow for two standard or king pillows per person; extras in a variety of shapes up the comfort factor and add a designer look.

COMFORT FACTORS
- *Firm* pillows offer maximum support and are perfect for back sleepers.
- *Medium* pillows offer a softer option while still retaining support for side sleepers.
- *Soft* pillows are generally lower height but with a soft feel. They are ideal for children and those who sleep on their tummy.

PILLOW FILLINGS

Feather and down pillows are the highest quality and softest pillows. They are filled with a mixture of white goose feather and white goose down. The feathers provide support while the down gives added softness and 'loft'. Ensure the down is goose, as duck down often has a slight odour.

A mix with more feathers provides support for back sleepers while a mix with more down is softer and better for stomach sleepers. Mixes (50/50) are good all-rounders.

Covers should be cotton ticking of no less than 230 thread count as sharp feather ends can break through. Pillow protectors should be used as this type of pillow can be difficult to clean.

Synthetic pillows are odourless, lofty, resilient and affordable. They are ideal if you prefer a reasonably firm pillow with the practicality of laundering.

Wool and wool-rich pillows are blended with synthetic fibres for firm support. They can be handwashed and dried naturally.

Latex pillows softly cradle your head and neck and come in various densities. Made from hypoallergenic rubber these pillows are a natural option for allergy sufferers and won't flatten or sag.

Foam pillows (also known as memory pillows) are popular as they provide good contoured support as well as retaining their shape.

COMMON PILLOW NAMES AND SIZES

- *European*   65cm x 65cm
- *King*   51cm x 91cm
- *Standard*   51cm x 66cm
- *Lumbar*   36cm x 91cm
- *Lumbar*   30cm x 61cm
- *Bolster*   25cm x 69cm
- *Square*   40cm x 40cm
- *Boudoir*   30cm x 40cm
- *Neck roll*   50cm x 14cm

PILLOW PROTECTORS

Using pillow protectors will help protect your pillows from soiling and staining, as well as assist in prolonging their life. Pillow protectors are also popular with allergy sufferers, as they can easily and regularly be washed. And they are excellent for using on children's pillows in case of sickness or little 'accidents'. But for the sake of freshness it makes sense to use them on all household pillows and throw them in the wash as often as necessary

QUILTS

Quilts with natural or synthetic fillings are soft, light and warm. The weight and price can vary with the type and amount of filling but this does not always indicate warmth. For an extra deep mattress, or if you prefer the quilt to hang a little further over the sides of the bed, buy a quilt one size larger than your mattress, for example a king size quilt for a queen size bed.

Feather and down-filled quilts are usually priced higher than the synthetic-filled quilts but do vary in feather and down type as well as content. Duck feather and down are among the more affordable and common types, but white goose is considered to be the best. In all feather and down mix quilts however, the higher the down content, the lighter and softer the quilt.

100% white goose down is the finest, softest and lightest of all quilt fillings. Goose down is the fluff from the belly of the goose and is an extremely efficient natural insulator. The lightest weight quilts are made from pure down and because it copes so well with temperature variations they can be used year round with comfort.

50/50 white goose feather and down are usually a more affordable option than pure white goose down. This mix of white goose feathers and down is also a practical alternative. The combination of down and feathers improves the warmth and softness of the quilt. The quilt cotton needs to be a feather proof ticking of at least 230 thread count to prevent feathers from poking through.

80/20 silver goose down and feather makes for a quilt lighter and softer than a 50/50 feather and down mix on account of the higher proportion of down. Grey goose down and feathers are also less expensive than white.

> **TIP** : *Buy two quilts and use the warmer quilt in winter and the cooler one in summer.*

Wool is another breathable, natural fibre that is warm in winter and cool in summer. Wool also absorbs moisture to give a restful sleep and is ideal for year-round use. A wool and synthetic blend combines the properties of wool with the loft of polyester, resulting in a durable and washable quilt.

Cotton is ideal for summer use and warmer climates as it is natural, breathable and machine washable.

Synthetic and micro fibres are available in summer and winter weights and are lofty, resilient, well priced and machine washable. Suitable for asthma and allergy sufferers, some have an anti-bacterial treatment to protect them from mould and mildew.

COMMON QUILT SIZES

- *Single*   140cm x 210cm
- *Double or twin*   180cm x 210cm
- *Queen*   210cm x 210cm
- *King*   245cm x 210cm
- *Super queen*   230cm x 240cm
- *Super king*   270cm x 240cm

BLANKETS AND THROWS

Light woollen and cotton blankets are year-round essentials. In summer I lie one over a sheet for the cooler morning hours; in winter it's reassuring to know a blanket's on stand by. A throw is more of a design accessory, best draped over the end of the bed in case it's needed or to add a dash of updating colour.

Woollen blankets are stylish, classic items you can own forever. They are soft and hard wearing – and are ideal for year-round comfort. Merino and lambswool make the softest woollen blankets. They are non prickly, breathable and flame retardant – perfect for babies and small children. Tufted woollen blankets have a high, light pile and are soft and fluffy with a springy texture.

Cotton cellular blankets are lightweight and great when it is too hot for a heavier blanket or quilt but too cool for just a sheet. The honeycomb-like weave allows maximum air circulation to efficiently regulate body temperature.

Synthetic and acrylic blankets are affordable and washable, but lacking in wool's quality, durability and warmth.

Chenille is made from plush, easy-care washable polyester or cotton and offers light warmth.

Fake fur looks incredibly luxurious and soft but is made from synthetic fibres rather than real fur.

Polyester fleece is warm, affordable and machine washable. Made from 100% polyester, it is suitable for lightweight throws for kids and comes in a wide range of colours.

Cashmere is a real luxury item and among the warmest, rarest and softest natural fibres in the world. It is ideal for babies' cot blankets and rugs.

SHEETS

Having a cupboard filled with stacks of odd sheets is not necessary when all you really need are a few well-made sets.

Quality sheets of light colour and design will give years of use plus the ability to mix and match easily. Purchasing several sets in the same colour is the best way I find to save time searching for the odd pillow case or sheet that may have become mixed up in the wash.

Sheets vary enormously in terms of what they are made from as well as quality, price and comfort. Always look for a high thread count and long staple fibre as these indicate how soft and long lasting the sheets will be. The number refers to how many threads have been woven into 10 square centimetres of cloth; the minimum quality should be around 230 thread count, even better is around 400, but the best can be up to 1000 thread count.

Staple refers to the length of the fibre, longer being softer, silkier and more lustrous. Egyptian, Pima and Upland cotton all have an excellent staple length and generally produce higher quality sheets.

Sheets are often sold in sets of a fitted sheet, flat or top sheet and two pillow cases in a standard size (one pair). Quilt covers and bed skirts are usually sold separately. Most manufacturers sell single sheets and pillow cases so you can stock up on extra items. The size of the bed linen you buy will depend on the individual sizes of your mattresses, pillows and quilts.

FLAT AND FITTED SHEETS

A bed needs to be made so it can be easily stripped, washed and remade once or twice per week. Use standard pillow cases for the pillows you sleep with, a fitted sheet with elasticised corners for a neat, smooth base and a flat sheet directly under the quilt or blankets. A flat sheet under the quilt is not everyone's choice but it does save washing – and water as well!

> **TIP** : *Deep-walled mattresses – 35cm, 40cm or 50cm – require larger fitted sheets.*

PILLOW CASES

Pillow cases (or shams) are sold in different styles and sizes so take care to check the packaging to ensure they will suit your pillow types.

They should have enveloped enclosures to prevent the pillow from being visible or slipping out.

STANDARD PILLOW CASE TYPES
- *Standard* plain or king size
- *European* which are large and square
- *Bordered or decorative*, often with flanged edges, either plain or ruffled

QUILT COVERS

For streamlined good looks and ease of handling covers should be purchased in exactly the same size as your quilts.

Select colours and styles which can be coordinated easily with your other bed linen. Simple styling and tones can easily be accessorised with bed throws and scatter cushions in contrasting or complementing colours.

A quilt cover should have firm enclosures such as buttons, velcro or zippers; an enveloped flap will give a neater appearance to the opening.

Ensure fabrics are easy care and machine washable.

BED SKIRT OR VALANCE

These are not essential, though generally ensemble or box spring based beds do look better when made with one.

A bed skirt can be tight and fitted for a modern look or loose with pleated corners for more traditional style. They can be purchased as a separate item with bed sheets and quilts and can also be custom made in fabric to match an upholstered head or curtains.

Ensure you buy the correct size to fit the dimensions of the bed base and that the skirt itself is long enough to cover bed legs and castors.

FABRICS FOR BED LINEN

There has never been a wider range of fabrics being made into bed linens. But what you choose will depend on a multitude of factors – whether you prefer the feel of natural or synthetic fabrics, how smooth you like your bed linen to look, how often you are likely to launder your bedding and, of course, what you can afford to spend.

Cotton sheets are my favourites. Perfect for any season, they always look fresh and are incredibly hard wearing. Like linen, they naturally 'breathe' and become softer with repeated use and washing. Being a natural fibre, cotton does tend to crush slightly but I think this adds to the softness and character of the fabric. If you like your sheets to look perfectly smooth you may prefer to use a cotton/polyester blend.

Egyptian cotton is an amazingly durable, lustrous and soft fabric which is well known to be one of the best qualities of sheeting available.

Combed cotton is widely available as sheeting. Combing separates the longer, smooth and strong cotton fibres from the short, resulting in a stronger fabric.

Percale is a term used for cotton sheeting with a strong, soft weave. Percale sheets can either be 100% cotton or a blend, usually 50/50 cotton/polyester.

In terms of quality, look for the highest thread count you can find. Whether cotton or a blend, the minimum should be around 230 thread count.

Sateen is made by weaving strong, long-fibred cotton to produce a shiny surface on the fabric giving a lustrous and smooth durable bed sheet which when washed will appear to lose its shine and silkiness. Ironing will smooth the fibres to regain the sheen of the fabric.

Cotton/polyester blends are a less expensive alternative to plain cotton and are a little easier to maintain because the polyester crushes less.

'Poly cotton' sheets have a smooth appearance even without ironing but will not 'breathe' as well as pure cotton so they may not be as comfortable for warm sleepers.

Jacquard or damask refers to subtle patterning in the cloth resulting from the way it has been woven. The shiny and flatter areas can give a beautiful dimension to otherwise plain sheeting. Available in cotton as well as blends.

Jersey is a soft and warm t-shirting fabric, just like the t-shirts you wear. Knitted jersey is not considered to be particularly long lasting as sheeting and is more of an affordable fashion item rather than an essential.

Flannelette is a loosely woven, heavy, soft cotton with a fuzzy finish. It varies in weight and texture and is a warm, cosy choice for winter. Especially good for children and those who like softer bedding.

Linen sheets are expensive but beautiful and the best choice for hotter climates. The fabric's natural tendency to absorb moisture and breathe keeps your body cool and dry. Linen becomes softer with use. Traditionally linen sheets were starched to make them appear crisp and smooth. However I prefer the natural soft appearance of freshly laundered linen straight from the clothes line, pressed with a hot iron.

Silk sheets, regrettably, are often expensive – but they are lovely and smooth to sleep on. Silk is graded as 'Momme' weight, with good silk sheeting being 18–19 'Momme'. Unfortunately silk sheets are very 'high maintenance', with most requiring hand washing or dry cleaning only. However being naturally hypoallergenic, silk may suit allergy sufferers.

Furnishings & accessories

The most comfortable bedrooms are those which
are furnished not only for sleeping, but also as a
retreat for relaxing, dressing and pampering
in complete peace and privacy.

ESSENTIALS
Wardrobe
Chest of drawers
Dressing mirror
Bedside cabinets/nightstands
Bedside lamps
Window treatments

GOOD TO HAVE
Rugs or carpeting
Heating &/or cooling
Bed head board
Chair (room permitting)
Dressing table & chair
Clothes basket
Alarm clock/radio

A bedroom should be a soothing, private and relaxing place, so when considering furnishings and colours, be guided not only by what is practical but also by what makes you – or those who sleep there – feel good.

If you are sharing a bedroom, compromise is the only way to ensure comfort for each person. Where possible, do what you can to agree on colours and furnishings, and exercise some degree of restraint to accommodate differing tastes.

When selecting a new decorating scheme, begin by making sure you have the key items of furniture for practicality and essential storage. While these don't have to be brand new or even matching, they should complement each other and be pleasing pieces to have.

For the classic bedroom, keep styling as simple as possible and select elegant shaping along with clean, fresh colours. It goes without saying that you should furnish the bedroom with the same attention to detail as you would any other room in the home. That way it can become a very personal retreat to enjoy, your own sanctuary from the world.

TIP : *Coordinate and update 'tired' bedroom furniture with paint, fabric and new hardware fittings.*

FURNITURE AND LIGHTING BASICS

The bedroom is your own private space so cherish this fully by taking the opportunity to furnish it in a more personal way than the rest of your home. Displaying wedding photographs, jewellery and special collections creates an intimate environment and allows you to fully enjoy things which could possibly look out of place anywhere else in the home.

WARDROBE

A wardrobe is necessary for organising and hanging clothes. Whether it is cabinet style or a walk-in room, it needs to be of a practical size to accommodate the clothes you regularly wear.

Clothes need enough hanging space for air to circulate freely around them. This reduces moisture build-up which causes damp and mildew. Excess moisture absorbers, cedar balls or bug strips, all available from the supermarket, should be used to prevent damp, moths and silverfish from ruining your clothes.

At the end of every season, clothes should be sorted, repaired and cleaned and things not needed for a while can be stored away to allow more hanging space.

CLOTHES HANGERS Having the correct clothes hangers is important to prevent clothes from becoming misshapen. It pays to invest in a variety of wooden, padded, fabric and clip style hangers.

- *Padded* hangers for delicate items.
- *Wooden* suit hangers for jackets and coats.
- *Clip* hangers for trousers and skirts.

SHOE STORAGE Shoes should be stored at the base of the wardrobe or on shelves if you have enough room in your wardrobe. To keep them neat and orderly, you could hang on to the boxes when you buy them or purchase clear plastic tubs to suit their sizes.

CHEST OF DRAWERS

Drawers should be deep and have smooth-running tracks. The style chosen should complement the bedroom.

Where space is limited a larger chest may be used as a bedside table and can be a great area for displaying photos and special items. Good organisation is the key to finding things, so sort each drawer according to clothing types and use drawer organisers to keep everything in its place and easy to find.

> **TIP** : *Keep the silica sachets which come with new shoes. These can be placed into the boxes when storing footwear to absorb dampness.*

DRESSING MIRROR

A long dressing mirror can be hung or floor standing. Perfect for introducing more light into the bedroom, a framed mirror in a bold size is both stylish and classic, whether in a traditional or more contemporary style.

BEDSIDE TABLES

Cabinets or small tables beside the bed are not only useful to hold lamps, clocks, water and books, but they also add balance and symmetry to the room.

Having said that, they don't have to match each other exactly, so long as they complement in the overall style and scheme. Better cabinet designs have cupboards as well as drawers which will encourage you to keep the table area clean and clear.

BEDSIDE LAMPS

Bedside lamps are essential for reading and to create balanced and intimate light. Choose sizes to suit the height of your bedside tables and shades to complement the room.

Bulbs should be around 40 watts; pearlised ones give a softer light.

An extra table or floor standing lamp is also a good idea for near a dressing table or reading chair.

WINDOW DRESSING

For most of us, covering bedroom windows is extremely important not only for privacy but so you can adjust light according to how and when you like to wake up. Some people prefer a blacked-out room while others like waking up with the sun. There are a number of window treatment options.

Curtains and drapes can be made with a maximum block-out backing which is designed to keep out the sun.

Sheer curtaining is often used for bedroom window privacy during the day. I prefer to use pure cotton instead of synthetic fibres to allow air to breeze through from the window.

Blinds can be used instead of or as well as curtaining for a different look but may allow light to filter between the blades and around the edges.

Shutters allow light and air to be filtered at various angles and will retain natural air flow in the room.

BEDROOM EXTRAS

Some things aren't essential by any means – but may make all the difference to your comfort.

BEDROOM CHAIR

A bedroom chair can be deep and cosy or simply a perch for tying your shoes. Either way, an upholstered chair will always be a practical bedroom addition and may present an escape from the busy house for a quiet read or contemplation.

DRESSING TABLE AND CHAIR

This kind of furniture may be considered a little old fashioned these days but I think a dressing table is a brilliant idea. It not only liberates the bathroom of make-up and hair-styling clutter but also provides an alternative dressing mirror, freeing the bathroom for the rest of the family.

HEADBOARDS

Headboards add real flair to a bedroom. They provide support when sitting up reading, and can also prevent pillows from slipping between the mattress and wall. Purchase headboards as part of the base, or separately.

Fabric or upholstered headboards should be cleanable and hard wearing and should coordinate with curtains and bedding. A removable slip cover is a practical option.

RUGS AND CARPETING

Some people like carpet in the bedroom for warmth under foot, while others prefer hard flooring to minimise dust and allergies. However, a thoroughly vacuumed carpet should present no real health risks and shouldn't be discounted entirely. Other natural options include sisal, coir or jute. Bedside rugs are an easy-care alternative to wall-to-wall carpeting.

HEATING AND COOLING

A reasonably constant temperature in the bedroom is vital for good sleep. In cooler weather, heaters on a low setting will remove the chill from the air. Don't over-heat the room or you'll wake feeling dehydrated.

Hot days and nights call for screened windows to be left open. An electric fan will circulate air around the room. Air-conditioning is another option.

CLOTHES BASKET

A deep, lidded laundry hamper will keep things tidy until wash day. A painted wicker basket is a smart option; a removable liner will protect clothing from catching on the sides. Wooden, fabric and plastic hampers and decorative wooden trunks are also useful.

ALARM CLOCK

Styles vary from battery-operated and wind-up clocks to digital ones. The alarm on any model will always be annoying!

OUTSIDE LIVING

Outdoor eating

They say, and I wholeheartedly agree, that food does actually taste
better when eaten outside. So, if you will pardon the pun,
take a leaf out of my book and find a suitable, sheltered area,
set up a table, chairs and barbecue and you will have the perfect excuse
to enjoy long lazy meals in the great outdoors.

When the weather is fine there's nothing lovelier than relaxing outdoors. Whether you have a balcony, patio, courtyard or sprawling garden, the simple yet affordable luxury of a set of comfortable chairs and a table large enough for all will make the world of difference to how you live.

Forget flimsy furniture which requires being put away after each use. Instead, opt for a sturdy outdoor setting – there's nothing like the convenience of having everything set up ready and waiting to be enjoyed.

Choose quality furniture framing made from hard-wearing materials which will stand up to years of use in harsh weather conditions. Cushioning should be the only part of the setting that needs to be stored or protected from the elements.

TIP : Place candles along an outdoor table in tall glass vases (with sand in the base) to protect their flames from the breeze.

Select a style that suits your home and garden, then place it in an inviting position, sheltered from the harsh sun and strong winds.

Well-considered planting will allow summer shade as well as winter sun and help create a protected area where family and friends can enjoy gatherings in comfort.

CHECKLIST

ESSENTIALS
- Table
- Chairs
- Umbrellas & shelter

GOOD TO HAVE
- Cushions & chair padding
- Barbecue
- Barbecue accessories
- Lighting
- Hurricane lamps
- Candles
- Mosquito repellents

OUTDOOR FURNITURE AND COOKING

Having quality outdoor furniture is essential for it to remain in good shape and stand up to the elements year after year. The designs and materials you choose should reflect the style of your home and sit well within the surroundings. They should also be durable and easy to maintain.

Timber furniture can be heavy, making larger chairs, tables and benches difficult to move around. Cedar, teak and mahogany are all highly durable out in the elements but need good care and regular maintenance to preserve them. Quality timbers are at the higher end of the price scale for outdoor furniture; however these will be more durable as well as resistant to warping and splitting.

Aluminium furniture is affordable and long lasting and is often sold in sets. The aluminium is often stylishly combined with glass and cushioning. Light and easy to carry as well as strong, and available in a wide range of colours and styles.

Plastic furniture is affordable and resistant to moisture but will fade and become brittle with age, especially when fully exposed to the elements. Stack and store or cover when not in use.

Cane furniture includes wicker, rattan and bamboo all of which are lightweight and good looking. Natural cane is not very durable when fully exposed to the elements however, so you may find that plastic coated or synthetic cane ends up being a better option.

Stone tables and benches can be expensive and incredibly heavy, but they do look amazing when positioned within a lush garden setting. Stone ages gently and often attracts mosses and lichens, giving it beautiful rustic appeal. Penetrating sealers may be used to give added protection to table tops; these should be available at hardware stores.

Wrought iron is often combined with timber, and can be long lasting and weather resistant if maintained regularly to prevent rust. The seats and backs should be padded, preferably with removable cushions.

CARE OF OUTDOOR FURNITURE

Clean outdoor furniture with warm soapy water and avoid harsh abrasive cleansers. Be sure to drain any water accumulated inside the frames before storing.

To prolong the life of outdoor furniture and cushions, store in a dry area out of the elements, or cover with furniture covers when not in use.

Cushions and padding fabrics need to be made from hard-wearing, weather-resistant materials such as acrylic or heavy cotton canvas. They need to be completely dry before storing to prevent mould and mildew.

ESSENTIAL SHADE

Umbrellas and other means of shading the garden are essential for enjoying outdoor meals and relaxing in comfort. Those fortunate enough to have tall trees or a vine-covered arbor or patio should take advantage of the cool canopy for perfect summer dining.

If you don't have trees, shade can be provided with a large umbrella, the span of which should cover the entire table. Weight and secure the poles for safety when it's breezy. The fabric should be thick enough to create total shade and durable enough to last for years. Heavy cotton canvas or acrylic are ideal.

Alternative shade solutions are shade sails (attached to the house) or permanent custom-made awnings.

> **TIP** : *Gauzy cotton panels are an ideal way to filter strong sunlight. These can be simply clipped to the edges of a portable umbrella using clothes pegs or stitched to make a more permanent 'tent'. Cotton fabric panels can easily be made and used as removable and washable outdoor curtains. Rods can be inserted through a pocket at the tops, then bracketed to the house eaves or pergola.*

BARBECUES

Having the facilities to cook outside means on warm days you can escape the heat of the kitchen and whip up quick and tasty meals which take no time at all.

Barbecues are also a great excuse to have friends over for a relaxed meal and everyone will be happy to gather around and chat while the cooking is being done.

Having two types of barbecue – a traditional, full-size and a portable – may seem extravagant but is definitely worthwhile if you enjoy long days outdoors or if you like to go camping.

When choosing a barbecue, the flavour of the food you enjoy the most, durability for your climate and aspect, plus the convenience of use are the most important factors to take into account.

TYPES OF BARBECUES

Charcoal grills or kettle barbecues give food a smoky flavour from the smouldering bed of hot coals. The kettle design is ideal for roasts. Most have adjustable vents so that you can regulate the flow of air and temperature of your fire. Smaller models are ideal for camping and picnics.

Gas grill barbecues heat quickly and are easy to start and shut down when the cooking is done. Most models can run on either cylinder or mains gas – which your plumber can connect for you so you will never run out of gas. Turn the isolator off when the barbecue is not in use.

Electric barbecue grills are convenient, compact and easy to use. This style is especially well suited for those with apartment balconies or townhouse courtyards where charcoal or gas barbecues may not be permitted.

Solid fuel/wood barbecues require some skill to control cooking temperatures but used with a cast iron plate or grill they will give the food a wonderful smoky flavour.

MATERIALS FOR BARBECUE HOTPLATES

A hotplate can be made from either porcelain-coated metal, cast iron or heavy brass and will be either flat or open grill style. Flat plates are better for onions, mushrooms and eggs while open grills allow fat to drain away from meats.

Cast iron is a particularly good conductor of heat, relatively easy to clean and very affordable. However if left exposed to the weather it is prone to rust and should never be washed with water.

Stainless steel hotplates are popular though more expensive than cast iron and not as good at conducting heat. They won't rust or absorb food smells but care needs to be taken with certain oils as they can burn easily and can be difficult to clean.

CLEANING A CAST IRON HOTPLATE Use a scraper to remove excess fat. The remaining thin film of fat on the plate will protect it and help prevent it from rusting.

The next time the barbecue is used, turn on high for a few minutes then down to low when you can wipe the surface over with a paper towel.

> **TIP** : *A cover will protect your barbecue from the weather and extend its lifetime, while a fat drip tray will protect your outdoor areas from oil.*

BARBECUE ACCESSORIES

Tools especially for the barbecue are quite different to those made for kitchen use and a set should be purchased and reserved for that purpose only. They need to be able to withstand high temperatures and exposure to the elements in case they are occasionally left outside and should be made from quality, long-lasting materials. Stainless steel is a good choice as it doesn't rust, and is durable and hygienic. Handles need to be longer than everyday kitchen tools and preferably flame resistant. I find the most useful items are a pair of tongs, a spatula, a cleaning scraper and a wire brush as well as a gas lighter or long matches.

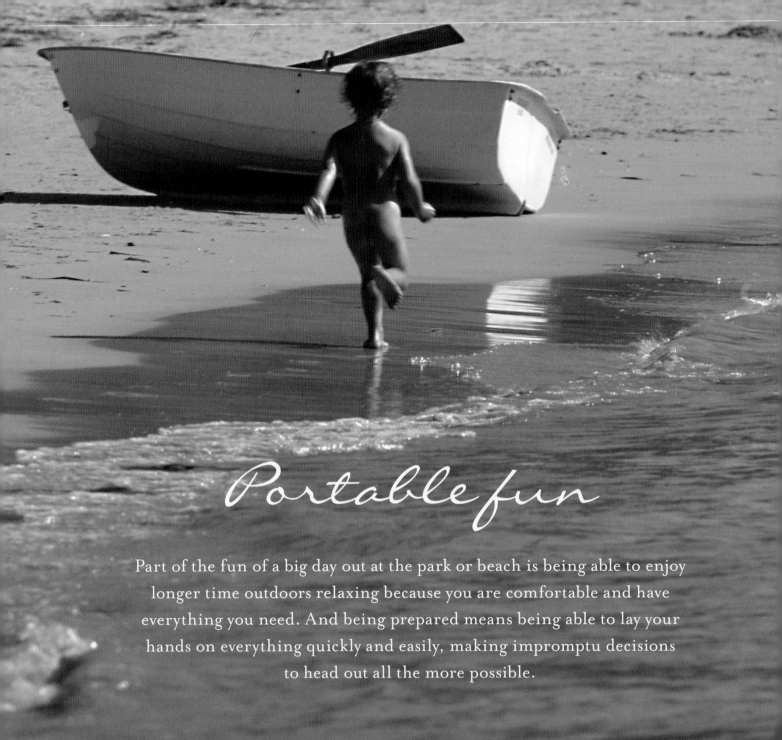

Portable fun

Part of the fun of a big day out at the park or beach is being able to enjoy longer time outdoors relaxing because you are comfortable and have everything you need. And being prepared means being able to lay your hands on everything quickly and easily, making impromptu decisions to head out all the more possible.

ESSENTIALS

- Picnic blanket
- Picnic basket
- Beach umbrella
- Esky
- Beach towels
- Sunblock cream
- Hats
- Sunglasses
- Swimwear
- Fold-up chairs

GOOD TO HAVE

- Portable tables & chairs
- Thermos flasks
- Portable barbecue & tools
- Portable wine carrier
- Cooler bags
- Beach carry basket
- Frisbee
- Cricket bat
- Kite
- Boogie board
- Snorkel & goggles
- Balls
- Boules
- Mini golf
- Bat & ball
- Beach toys

Having furniture and accessories which are portable as well as practical makes a lot of sense to me because if you can take the conveniences of being at home with you, a day spent outdoors can be as luxurious and comfortable as you like.

Now, I am not exactly what you would call the overly adventurous type, but I don't mind getting away from it all, so long as I can be surrounded with a few creature comforts. Essentials like a thermos for tea and coffee may seem a little old fashioned but certainly are great when a café is not within walking distance. An esky cooler makes gourmet meals more than feasible. And with a blanket and book thrown in, what more could you need for a civilised day outdoors?

TIP : *Having a colour scheme in mind when buying new picnic items helps not only to make selection easier but gives a stylish, coordinated look.*

To maximise time available for having fun outside, it's well worth preparing ahead of time and having the essentials ready and waiting. Rather than raiding your kitchen cupboards, set up a picnic basket or hamper. Keep it clean, organised and well stocked and, most importantly, easy to access. All you then need do is add some food and drink and you're ready to go!

PORTABLE FURNITURE AND PICNIC EQUIPMENT

Picnic tables and chairs are such an affordable luxury for relaxing and eating in comfort when out for the day. Choose ones that are lightweight, durable and easy to fold and carry. Most styles are reasonably compact, so they can be stored easily in the shed or garage. Hanging them on strong wall brackets keeps them within easy reach and they can be packed into the car quickly with minimum fuss.

Tables with a luggage-style carry handle are best. Those which fold out save time but also need to have leg bracing for strength. Compact designs which fold in half save car and storage space.

Aluminium chairs with easy-care polyester seating are ideal for outdoor events, sporting matches and fishing. Styles range from quick-folding stools to the more elaborate chairs with backs and arm rests, drink pouches and zippered pockets. Look for compact styles which fold flat or bunch tightly into carry bags.

Deck and director's chairs with canvas seating are stylish and comfortable but not as portable. They are more suited for anywhere they don't have to be carried too far. The canvas will rot and perish if the chairs are left in the weather or stored in a damp shed and regular maintenance of the timber will be needed to keep it in good condition.

Picnic blankets should be waterproof with a sturdy nylon underside to protect from any dampness on the ground. Some styles have a bag or tote with an adjustable shoulder strap for easy carrying. Car blankets made from polar fleece are lightweight and easy to wash.

Thermos flasks are very useful, especially on cold days. Wider styles are great for hot, comforting soups.

Portable barbecue and tool sets are handy for picnics and all you need to cook up a storm.

Thermal drink carriers or drink pouches keep bottles cool and safe when carrying. Look for easy-clean fabrics with secure enclosures and carrying straps.

Cooler bags should be fully insulated with removable liners for easy care and long handles for shoulder carrying.

Eskies are insulated boxes suitable for storing cool foods. All sizes will need to have a sturdy outer casing with strong carry handles on the sides. Lids can be completely removable or hinged; a latch will improve sealing and secure contents while on the move. Models with taps allow any melted ice to be drained easily.

STOCKING A PICNIC BASKET   Choose a basket style which is portable, has a secure handle and can be cleaned, maintained and stored easily. To stock your own permanent picnic basket, you will need:

- Glasses – plastic is durable
- Forks, knives and spoons, stainless steel
- Vacuum flask
- Cutting board, wood with juice grooves
- Set of spill-proof salt and pepper shakers
- Water-resistant blanket
- Plates, unbreakable
- Insulated cups, brushed stainless steel
- Napkins, cotton
- Corkscrew, stainless steel
- Wine stopper
- Plastic food containers with lids
- Insulated wine/drink pouch, canvas
- Plastic bags for rubbish and dirty utensils
- Zip-lock bags for left-overs

HOME CARE

Laundry equipment

To prolong the life of your home and keep all your belongings in good working order, a system of regular care and maintenance is needed. Housework can be dull, so the main objective is to get it over and done with as quickly and efficiently as possible and with the best results.

ESSENTIALS

- Washing machine
- Vacuum cleaner
- Buckets
- Washing & polishing cloths
- Sponges & scourers
- Soft floor broom
- Brush & pan set
- Mop
- Floor scrubbing brush
- Toilet brush
- Pegs
- Clothes baskets
- Clothes hangers
- Clothes hamper
- Clothes line
- Iron
- Ironing board
- Garbage bin liners
- First aid kit

GOOD TO HAVE

- Product, equipment & linen storage
- Clothes dryer
- Clothes airer
- Dry cleaning bags
- Stiff bristled floor broom
- Cobweb broom
- Steel wool

We all like clean, comfortable surroundings but no-one wants to be a slave to them, so establishing efficient systems of care and maintenance should be a priority. For busy homes, regular tidying and cleaning makes more sense than letting a big mess build up until things get out of hand. Doing just a few small jobs each day doesn't take much time and makes all the difference for staying on top of things and keeping the home running smoothly.

The laundry room is a like a mini maintenance department, and as such should be fully equipped with all of the bits and pieces needed to keep everything in your home in tip-top working order. While you don't need every product or gadget on the market, you do need a good selection of effective tools and materials to take care of housework without too much expenditure of precious time and energy. Select machines and products according to their ease of use and versatility.

Good laundry storage is also necessary, with cupboards and shelves organised to allow equipment to be seen and accessed easily. Care should be taken with poisonous and hazardous chemical products; always store them safely and securely away from small children and pets – preferably in lockable cupboards.

LAUNDRY DESIGN

Although the laundry is primarily used for cleaning clothes and storing equipment, it doesn't have to look utilitarian. Functional and practical can be attractive too! It's just a matter of giving some long and clear thought to how you store and display things. When refurbishing or designing a new laundry, consider the layout carefully. Given careful planning and attention to detail, the laundry can easily be as smart as other busy rooms in the house.

Keep surfaces as streamlined as possible and select materials for their ease of care and cleaning. Do consider built-in cabinets with doors in a similar style to kitchen cabinetry and allow enough floor area for a clothes hamper. A deep bench is useful for folding clothes as well as storing laundry baskets and the iron while it cools. Shelves can accommodate clear jars of pegs and detergents while a few wall hooks are handy for bags, leads and hangers.

> **TIP** : *Make sure laundry cabinets and benches are made from waterproof materials which will stand up to harsh cleaning chemicals.*

Simple white is always a good colour choice for tiles and work surfaces as it coordinates so well with laundry appliances. Brighter colours can be introduced to paintable wall areas away from the sink and splash zone.

TILES

The laundry is primarily a wet area so tiling the floor and walls is a practical option. The floor should be fully tiled while the walls can be partially covered, mainly around the sink and work spaces. Glazed ceramic tiles will stand up to cleaning products and can be wiped down easily. Floor tiles should be chosen for their grip as well as their ability to be cleaned.

SINK

Regardless of a laundry sink being cabinet style or bench top, it must be deep enough to be able to fill buckets easily. Stainless steel not only looks sleek but is easy to keep hygienically clean.

TAPS AND SPOUT

There's no need for any fancy fittings in the laundry, but taps should be easy to turn on and off with wet hands. Look for a simple design that will be a breeze to wipe clean.

The laundry spout needs to be long enough to reach over the largest bucket. Modern styles have retractable hoses which are perfect for all kinds of chores.

CABINETS AND BENCHES

Ideally these should be made from waterproof materials which will also stand up to harsh cleaning chemicals. Fitted base or wall cabinets save space and provide excellent storage

> **TIP** : *Child proof safety latches or locks should be fitted to base cabinets containing poisonous chemicals.*

while floor to ceiling cabinetry can even conceal a laundry area entirely. Many kitchen flat-pack cupboards suit a laundry environment and are an economical way to fit out the room yourself. Alternatively, a cabinet maker can custom-build to your specifications.

VENTILATION

Good ventilation is a must in the laundry to prevent it becoming musty. Open windows frequently and let the room air properly.

If you regularly use a clothes dryer, consider having it ducted to prevent moisture build-up.

HOUSEHOLD LINEN AND TOWEL STORAGE

A cupboard with plenty of clean, smooth shelves is perfect for storing towels and linen. Make sure things aren't too crammed in as fabric needs plenty of air circulating freely around it to prevent dampness. Organise your sheets in sets for each bed in the house, rather than piles. That way you will save time in searching for the odd pillow case at bed-making time. Sorting the towels according to size and type will make it easier to find what you're after when you're in a hurry too.

CLEANING EQUIPMENT

Wash-day and general household chores become far less onerous when you've got the right equipment for the job.

WASHING MACHINE

Deciding on a top loading or front loading washing machine comes down to personal choice as well as your laundry layout. Each has its own advantages and should be considered carefully for washing capacity, duration of cycles, water usage as well as range of settings. For a large family, it's worth considering the largest capacity machine available and even going to the expense of an industrial model. This is one appliance I really do feel is worth investing significantly in for quality – simply because of the vast amount of work it will do in its lifetime as well as how carefully it will treat and wash your clothes.

- *A top loading machine* will need plenty of space for opening the lid. When closed can double-up as extra bench space.
- *A front loading machine* can slide in under a bench and may also have a dryer stacked on top. It is generally a better choice where space is limited.

> TIP : *Adequate ventilation is essential in a laundry. If you regularly use a clothes dryer consider having it ducted to prevent moisture build-up.*

CLOTHES LINE

A garden washing line should be sized according to how much laundry you do. If you are like me – 'Dame Wash-a-lot' – and do many loads each week, it will need to be large enough to accommodate plenty! A useful guide is enough line space for several wide bed sheets and a few baskets of smaller items.

- Retractable and removable clothes lines give you the freedom to remove them, freeing up backyard space for play and entertaining.
- An internal line is useful for overnight airing and lightweight drying of small items – and the ideal place for it is in your laundry, attached to a wall.

CLOTHES AIRER

A fold away clothes airer is good to have for rainy days or winter or for those without a garden or enough space for a washing line. Plastic coated rungs are easy to wipe over but should be replaced if the coating becomes damaged as the metal framing will usually rust and stain clothing.

CLOTHES DRYER

A clothes dryer is useful to have for airing and drying clothes during damp weather or if you have no outside drying facility. Be aware that they can cause shrinkage with certain fabrics and are unsuitable for drying delicates.

A choice of settings is useful – cool for airing, medium for partial drying and hot for thorough drying.

IRONING BOARD

I find it useful to have two ironing boards. A conventional, portable, free-standing, regular ironing board has a long and wide surface for tablecloths and larger jobs. A cupboard-mounted style is convenient and compact – perfect for those quick, last minute presses.

The ironing board cover should be clean and padded and replaced if it becomes stained or damaged. It should sit securely and smoothly on the board and have reflective lining to help cut down ironing time.

IRON

If you've ever gone out and worried about having left the iron on, consider one of the new irons with the ability to turn itself off if it hasn't been used within 15 minutes.

Self-cleaning steam irons are also now available, and they're a real bonus given the range of clothing fabrics now available. A wider variety of settings means you can safely iron all sorts of natural and synthetic fabrics without scorching them.

I like a clear reservoir to see when the water is running low. A non-stick plate helps the iron glide along smoothly.

VACUUM CLEANER

A good quality vacuum cleaner is essential, regardless of the type of flooring you have. Detachable nozzles and brushes are designed for sofas, cushions and upholstery as well as window blinds, bed mattresses and curtains. The best vacuum cleaners have strong power, and don't lose suction. Look for those with the highest suction wattage and consider if you want one with or without removable bags and filters. A vacuum should be fairly lightweight and easy to move around, particularly if you have different floor levels or stairs.

BROOMS AND BRUSHES

A variety of brushes are needed for different tasks – everything from cleaning floors and toilets to general household chores and spring cleaning.

- Soft floor and stiff bristled floor brooms
- Mop
- Cobweb broom
- Dust pan and brush
- Toilet brush
- Floor scrubber
- Pot scrubber

BUCKETS

Start a small collection of sizes and colour code them for specific uses. The handles should be substantial for comfortable and safe carrying when the bucket is full.

CLOTHS, SPONGES AND SCOURERS

- Washing cloths which can be laundered are strong and will last the longest.
- Old tea towels and face washers are ideal when dusting and polishing.
- Scourers are an absolute must for the tough jobs. You can buy specific ones for different surfaces.
- Keep a sponge and chamois leather just for car cleaning.

GARBAGE BIN LINERS

Indispensable for keeping bins fresh. Help look after the environment by choosing degradable ones or re-use supermarket shopping bags.

Buy garbage bin liners in a number of different strengths and sizes. You're bound to find uses for them in every room.

PAPER TOWEL

Always good to have on hand for mopping up all sorts of really messy spills. Consider mounting a dispenser on the laundry wall so it's handy when little accidents happen.

STEEL WOOL

Not used so often in these days of 'specialist' scourers, but still very useful when some real 'elbow grease' is required.

FIRST AID KIT

Every home should have a well stocked first aid kit. Keep it well out of reach of children, but accessible for when it's needed.

You can stock it yourself, or buy one ready assembled. Essentials include bandaids in various shapes and sizes, a range of gauze bandages, disinfectant, cotton wool, antiseptic cream, tweezers (for splinters) and a thermometer.

Replace items as necessary or if past their use-by date.

LAUNDRY TIPS

- Pegs can rot and perish so make sure you remove them from the clothes line and store them inside.
- Clothes baskets can be of wicker or plastic but need to have sturdy handles for carrying heavy loads of wet washing.
- A clothes hamper with compartments saves time sorting clothing into lights, coloureds and darks.
- Dry cleaning bags will store your articles of clothing safely until dry cleaning-day.
- Clothes hangers which are plastic coated and padded are ideal for drying lightweight items.

Cleaning products

Supermarkets are filled with an enormous range of cleaning products, all with different smells, packaging and claims — but I find the most basic cleaners are often still the best. These ones are my favourites and over years I have found them to be the most consistently reliable to get the jobs done.

HOME CLEANING

Cleaning the house regularly is essential to keep it looking good and to maintain a healthy environment. Dust mites, mould, pet hair and general dirt are all unpleasant and can cause harmful allergies. With a little commonsense and a few basic products, your house can always be fresh and clean.

Open as many windows as possible every day. It's even better if you can open windows on opposite sides of the house to create a flow-through breeze.

Your nose is usually the best indicator of when it's time to clean. Damp smells indicate more ventilation is required; musty odours can be eliminated by regular dusting and vacuuming. Some cleaning tasks do require mild chemicals but if you or your family find them irritating, look for natural, mild or low-irritant products.

Generally, simple products will take care of most jobs. Limiting your range of cleaning essentials will save storage space – and allow you to become familiar with the chemical constituents of each and how best to use them.

> **TIP** : *Never mix chemical cleaners as reactions may occur. Use them only according to the directions on the labels.*

CHECKLIST

ESSENTIALS

Laundry detergent

Wool wash

Soap flakes

Dishwashing liquid

Pure soap

Household bleach

Antibacterial cleaners

Toilet gel cleaner

Nappy soak

Paste cleanser

Oven cleaner

Furniture polish

Window cleaning spray

White vinegar

Borax

Bicarbonate of soda

GOOD TO HAVE

All-purpose spray cleaner

Carpet cleaner

Antiseptic

Washing soda

HOME CLEANING ESSENTIALS

Before using any commercial cleaning products, always read the labels to make sure they won't cause damage.

Cleaning products can also be harsh on the skin so rubber gloves should be worn – or rinse your hands well after use. Fumes, particularly from bleaches and solvents can be harmful so only use those products in well-ventilated areas.

All-purpose spray cleaner has a multitude of cleaning uses in just about every room in the home.

Antibacterial cleaners & antiseptics assist with keeping household germs at bay.

Bicarbonate of soda mixed with a few drops of water forms a paste which cuts through light grease and oil and is useful as a mild abrasive.

Borax powder is a water softener and general disinfectant; good for boosting laundry detergent and for soaking nappies.

Carpet cleaner is specifically designed for cleaning laid carpets. Make sure you follow the manufacturer's directions.

Dishwashing liquid is a mild, perfumed detergent which should be diluted with water for general cleaning.

Furniture polish is a perfumed spray that adds shine and lustre to timber furniture.

Household bleach can be used for cleaning and brightening, disinfecting, removing mould and mildew, as well as effective stain removal.

Laundry detergents are available in either liquid or powder form and are designed for use with washing machines.

Nappy soak is a mild form of bleach which contains softeners and detergents and is useful for gently soaking and cleaning white fabrics.

Oven cleaners are extremely harsh and should be used with care. Make sure there is plenty of ventilation when using; rubber gloves are essential.

Paste cleanser is useful as a mild abrasive for general cleaning but you need to be careful not to damage the surface being cleaned. Bicarbonate of soda mixed with a little water also makes a good paste cleanser.

Pure soap may seem a little old-fashioned but a bar of it will come in very handy. Useful for rubbing at stains and soil marks before tossing clothes into the washer.

Soap flakes are made from 100% pure soap and are useful for washing delicate fabrics like wool and silk.

Spray stain removers help with general staining and should be sprayed on prior to washing.

Toilet cleaner is a thick, gel cleaner which often contains bleach and descaling agents for use in the toilet bowl.

White vinegar can be used with washing soda and hot water to clear a blocked drain. A capful added to window or floor washing water will also add shine.

Window cleaning spray should be used with a dry, lint-free cloth to remove marks from glass and mirrors.

Wool wash is gentle and should be used instead of regular laundry detergents for washing wool and delicate fabrics. Alternatively, pure soap flakes my be used.

Odd jobs

Every home needs a few well stocked kits for any odd jobs which
need attending to. Organise kits separately into individual task boxes,
that way everything will be close at hand and easy to find.

ODD JOBS KITS

Even if you are challenged in the 'do it yourself' department, from time to time you may need to try your hand at a few minor repairs or adjustments. Small jobs which don't warrant calling out the experts may need just a little attention. So whether or not you're a home handyperson, having a few basic, well-stocked odd jobs kits will serve you well and see you through many an 'emergency' task.

Store odd job tools and equipment in an orderly fashion. See-through plastic carry cases or containers with compartments are great for immediate identification. Group your bits and pieces according to the tasks they are used for – say, picture hanging, sewing and clothing repairs, shoe and leather care, or fuse replacement.

If possible, try to keep odd job kits close at hand too. You don't want to be traipsing about looking for them or having to get up and down to high shelves or cupboards. Keep them where you can put your hands on them at a moment's notice.

TIP : Ensure tools always go back to their kits as soon as you have finished the task at hand. That way things will always be ready when you need them.

CHECKLIST

ESSENTIALS
Hammer
Hand saw
Level
Long-nosed pliers
Staple gun
Screw driver set
Box of assorted screws & nails
Picture hooks
Electrical extension lead
Power point double adaptors
Spare light bulbs
Tape measure
Drop sheet
Step ladder
Utility knife & spare blades
Scissors
Shoe polish & brushes

GOOD TO HAVE
Cordless drill
Drill bits
Pliers
Wire cutters
Assorted string & cord
Masking tape
Picture hooks
Picture wire
Sewing needles & pins
Thread in assorted colours
Spare buttons
Sewing machine
Shoe travel bags

SMALL HANDY TOOLS

For minor maintenance and repairs, I find it so helpful to have a portable carry case stocked with a set of basic, reliable tools. These can be bought over time and added to as needed, but a few items like screw drivers, a hammer, a level and some pliers are a good start. A jar of screws and nails is always helpful, along with a tape measure, utility knife and hand saw. Space permitting, a small, fold-up step ladder is useful; it can be hung on a wall when not in use.

An electrical kit can also be good to have. Use it to store extension leads, plug adapters, power boards and electrical tape. Spare light bulbs and batteries are always useful, as are torches in a variety of sizes.

PICTURE HANGING

When feeling inspired, I•do tend to start hanging pictures at odd hours and am always grateful when I can lay my hand on hooks, wire and a hammer without having to go searching. A small kit for picture hanging takes up hardly any room at all. It should also contain a spirit level, pencil, staple gun, tape and BluTac.

TIP : Once a picture is hung, to keep it hanging straight, press a small piece of BluTac to the back of the frame where it touches the wall.

SEWING AND REPAIRS

For those last minute emergency clothing repairs, a small box of sewing items is definitely worth having. Begin with a few needles, cotton, a pair of scissors and some spare buttons.

For larger sewing jobs, an extended kit should, at the very least, contain a measuring tape, needles, cottons in various colours, pins, safety pins, a laundry marker for labelling clothing and a good, sharp pair of fabric scissors. A basic sewing machine as well is a great idea and not only saves money with home

TIP : Sewing kits which hotels supply to guests are perfect for minor fabric repairs as the needles are already threaded in a variety of colours.

furnishings but also allows unique touches to be added.

When sewing by hand, the most useful and common needles are known as 'sharps'. These range in length and sizes from coarse to fine. The general rule of thumb is the finer the fabric, the finer the needle required. Embroidery or crewel needles are exactly like sharps but have a longer eye for easier threading. Tapestry needles are generally thicker with a blunt or ball point end which is ideal for sewing knitted and elastic fabrics without tearing the threads.

SHOE AND LEATHER CARE

To keep leather shoes and hand bags looking their best and in good condition, regular cleaning and polishing is needed. Set up a shoe shine box, stock it with polish, brushes and cloths and store it within easy access for a quick dust and polish when needed.

TIP : Use old t-shirts or towelling for shoe polishing cloths. Always spread newspaper on the floor to protect it from polish.

A standard shoe care kit should always have wax polish or shoe cream in colours of black, brown and neutral. Clear water-proofing wax is also useful for boots and leather requiring extra protection from the elements.

Horse hair brushes are the best for applying wax polish. Use one each for black, brown and blue and use spares for other colours. They should be kept specifically for applying wax; use separate brushes for polishing and shining.

Shoe wipes or a quick-shine sponge are great to have for last minute polishes or when travelling. When packing for holidays, place shoes into cloth drawstring shoe bags. This keeps them not only protected but also saves polish or dirt from affecting other garments in your suitcase.

For leather and suede furnishings, carefully follow the manufacturer's directions when cleaning or polishing. Some retailers can also advise about this, but if in any doubt contact the maker's customer line direct. Many manufacturers also have information-packed websites.

Garden maintenance

Whether you have a green thumb or not, every home with a garden
needs a basic selection of tools in order to keep the area around your
home looking tidy and well cared for.

ESSENTIALS

Hand trowel

Spade

Fork

Secateurs

Watering can

Garden hose

Brooms

Dust pan & brush

Gloves

Twine

GOOD TO HAVE

Lawn mower

Lawn edger

Brush cutter

Shovel

Rakes

Garden hoe

Pick

Hedge clippers

Pruning saw

Wheelbarrow

Garden scissors

Bamboo stakes

THE PLEASURES OF GARDENING

I think gardening must be a rite of passage and it seems the older I become, the more I enjoy having a potter around in the soil. Despite gardening being hard work at times, I will admit there is something very healing and special about spending the day digging, pruning and weeding out in the fresh air.

The garden always seems so appreciative of any effort spent on it, even just mowing the lawn and cleaning up the path edges. It can really tidy things up and make the world of difference to the appearance of your home.

On a design note, I can't stress enough the value that some well selected and positioned plants, trees and shrubs can add not just in terms of structure and form but also of adding interest and colour as well as ensuring privacy.

So whether or not you have a 'green thumb', every home with a garden — however small — will benefit from a basic gardening plan and routine in order to maximise its appearance and keep the plants healthy.

TIP : *A set of quality gardening hand tools — and perhaps a mat to kneel on while weeding and transplanting — makes a lovely gift for any gardener.*

GARDENING TOOLS AND MAINTENANCE

The size and weight of gardening tools should make chores like digging and pruning comfortable. Certain tools come in a variety of sizes and some will be easier to manage than others so don't be afraid to try them out in the shop and compare what feels best for you. Where possible, use tools with forged heads for strength. And for cutting blades, stainless steel ones are the best.

Keeping your tools clean and sharp will extend their life so make sure you take a minute to clean off any mud or sap before storing them away in a dry shed or cupboard out of the weather. Spades, hoes and clippers need to be sharpened once a year with a file or sharpening stone. Wooden handled tools should be rubbed with linseed oil to keep them nourished and to prevent splinters.

SPADE

For digging, chopping, lifting and edging.

FORK

A steel fork will be easier than a spade to break up the soil before planting.

SHOVEL

A shovel is for moving soil, sand and gravel.

GARDEN HOE

Choose a hoe with a long, comfortable handle for weeding and ploughing the soil.

PICK

For removing tufty roots and breaking up heavy soil.

RAKES

Metal rakes are for smoothing soil and gravel. Plastic splayed rakes are for raking leaves and lawn clippings.

SECATEURS

Short-handled secateurs are for pruning home-grown fruit, vegetables, flowers and shrubbery. Long-handled loppers are for thin tree and shrub branches.

HEDGE CLIPPERS

Wavy blades are for clipping thick shrubbery. Straight blades are for finer foliage and grass.

PRUNING SAW

Makes light work of pruning that is too tough for secateurs.

WHEELBARROW

A wheelbarrow should feel comfortable to push with a full load as well as be sturdy and durable.

GARDEN HOSE

A hose which constantly kinks can be very annoying and the cheaper vinyl types are the ones most likely to do it. Look for a heavier weight rubber and vinyl mix hose or for the best quality choose pure rubber. The length should be suitable to reach from the tap to the furthest point in your garden.

TROWEL

A hand trowel is necessary for small planting jobs, weeding, mixing and fertilising.

BROOMS

A wide millet broom is better for sweeping concrete and pavers, while a soft-headed brush broom for is for sweeping decking, steps and doorways. Use a stiff-bristled decking broom with water to scrub timber boards.

DUST PAN AND BRUSH

Use a wide pan and large brush for the garden. Make sure it is of sturdy construction.

LAWN MOWERS

The kind of lawnmower you need will most likely depend on how much grass you have to cut, the type of lawn, how quickly it grows and needs mowing, and how fond you are of raking up the clippings!

PETROL   Conventional petrol mowers with catchers which collect the grass for disposal or composting are the popular choice for the average suburban lawn. They are usually powered by a 2- or 4-stroke engine. The 2-stroke engines require oil to be added to the petrol, while 4-strokes take standard petrol and the oil is contained in a separate part of the engine much like a car. And like a car, 4-stroke engines require a regular oil change. These mowers are generally started with a pull cord, however, some of the more expensive models are available with an electric ignition.

FLYMO   Flying or hovering type lawn mowers have no wheels and are easy to use as they hover just above the lawn on a cushion of air. The cutting blades perform two functions, cutting as well as providing the force to lift the mower off the ground.

> TIP : *Always abide by any water restrictions that may be in place.*

ELECTRIC   Plug-in electric lawn mowers are convenient for small lawns where it will be easy to run a power lead without causing inconvenience. As with all mowers, be careful when using and take extra precautions when children are about.

LAWN EDGERS

Lawn edgers are used to trim round the edges of the grassed areas of your yard. Great if you have lots of garden beds, lengthy pathways or a long driveway.

BRUSH CUTTERS

Brush cutters (or whippersnippers) are ideal for trimming along edges, fences or areas where the lawn mower won't reach.

GLOVES

Knitted wrist bands will keep out the dirt and leather palms will give extra protection. Cotton backing makes the gloves cool and flexible.

TWINE

Natural jute is pliable and kind on young plants when tying and training them on supports. Always handy to have a large roll of it on hand.

GARDEN SCISSORS

These have a multitude of uses around the garden. A utility pair in stainless steel will prove very useful. Make sure you have them sharpened regularly.

BAMBOO STAKES

Cheap, strong and able to withstand the weather, these come in very handy for supporting young trees and shrubs as well as in the vegetable garden.

Painting essentials

One of the fastest ways to transform a piece of furniture, wall, room or entire house is with paint — and the job can be made so much easier and fun if you have the right equipment. Buying the best paints, brushes and tools you can afford makes great sense, not only in terms of saving time but for the professional results you will achieve. Consider your decorating equipment an investment and look after it well; that way you are always prepared for any rainy weekend of decorating.

CHECKLIST

ESSENTIALS

- Paint
- Paint brushes
- Paint rollers
- Roller frames
- Paint trays
- Drop cloths
- Masking tape
- Filler
- Filling knives & scrapers
- Sanding blocks & paper

GOOD TO HAVE

- Paint tray liners
- Roller extension poles
- Paint mixing paddle
- Sugar soap
- Turpentine
- Ladder

PAINT

Take my advice and never skimp on paint quality. Less expensive brands are often thin and have less colour coverage, and this only means having to apply more coats to achieve a good finish.

The type of paint you apply to interior walls and ceilings is different to that for woodwork, trims and doors. Exterior paints are different again so make sure you check the paint is suitable for your application before purchasing.

The most common type of paint used for interiors is water based acrylic, available in a wide range of colours and in a number of sheen levels. Matt is popular for ceilings whereas low to mid sheen is a good choice for walls.

TIP : Specialty finishes in contemporary paint ranges also include suede, pearlescent and metallics. Try a sample pot before buying in quantity.

Woodwork like doors and architraves requires a different paint from walls – either acrylic or oil based enamel in a matt, semi gloss or gloss finish. Despite the yellowing associated with oil based paints and their stronger odour when applying, I prefer their application and durability to that of water based woodwork paints.

PAINTING EQUIPMENT

The initial outlay on quality equipment is well worth it.

PAINT BRUSHES

The best paint brushes are made using high quality synthetic filament bristles which won't fall out and get left behind in your work. Synthetic bristles are relatively easy to clean and can be used for either water or oil based paints. Choose a width to suit your grip as well as the size of the job.

PAINT ROLLERS

Try to resist buying the cheap paint roller kits if you want a quality paint finish. The best rollers actually make the job easier in the long run as they deliver the paint more evenly resulting in better coverage.

The best paint rollers are made from lambswool and mohair and being natural fibres are easier to clean than synthetic roller sleeves. Roller sleeves are made in varying thicknesses or naps to suit smooth or rough surfaces.

PAINT ROLLER FRAMES

These need to be sturdy. The part that slips into the roller sleeve needs to remain clean so it will spin easily. Clean them well after each use to prevent paint clogging.

> **TIP** : Paint tray liners, being disposable, save time and water at clean up.

PAINT TRAYS

It's important that the trays should suit the width of the painting rollers you are using. Some have a 'hook' for hanging the tray off the rung of a ladder.

ROLLER EXTENSION POLES

As far as I'm concerned these are the only way to paint walls and ceilings quickly and easily. I use a lightweight aluminium pole which screws into the end of a roller frame and extends to around 3 metres if needed.

PAINT MIXING PADDLES

Essential for mixing paint colour thoroughly. I use long wooden sticks which can be used later as sample swatches to match with fabrics and furniture.

DROP CLOTHS

Thick, heavyweight cotton canvas is my preferred choice as plastic tends to be slippery. Canvas cloths are tightly woven to protect floors while you are working but are not impervious to big paint spills so care still needs to be taken to avoid splashes and puddles where you need them least. Plastic drop cloths (which you can buy at paint shops) are generally fine for keeping paint off the floor when tackling small paint jobs.

MASKING TAPE

For masking windows, doors and walls while painting. It comes in a variety of different tack levels. I use a low to medium tack which is not so sticky as to remove the surface layer underneath. Tape should be firmly pressed down to prevent paint from bleeding and the roll should never be left in the sun or damp or it will be rendered as useless.

FILLER

Must be purchased to suit different surfaces. For water based paints and stains you should use water based fillers, otherwise the paint may have difficulty in adhering properly. For oil-based paints use fillers with an oil base.

Filling knives and scrapers are helpful for any preparation jobs requiring a flat, broad blade. Care should be taken not to gouge the wall with the corners of the blades.

SANDING BLOCKS AND PAPER

These are essential to provide a scuffed surface which help give subsequent coats of paint a good surface to stick to. Failure to sand can cause paint to peel. I use glass rather than sandpaper and never use coarse which is too damaging to the surface.

MATERIALS GUIDE

LFY-22756F
Horizontal: 27" (68 cm) - Vertical: Random
54" (137 cm)
LP
100% Cotton
Belgium

FABRICS

ACRYLIC is used extensively in home furnishings for its relatively low price, ease of care and durability. Often used as a substitute for wool, acrylic is sometimes blended with cotton to resist creasing and shrinkage. Common uses include blankets, sheeting, curtains and carpet.

BROCADE is a highly decorative silk, cotton or rayon fabric with a slightly raised pattern, often of flowers, scroll work and scenes. Suitable for elegant, formal upholstery, curtains and cushions.

CALICO is made from pure cotton and is often used as a cost-effective curtain or lining fabric. Fabric widths and qualities vary according to the intended use. Generally available in a creamy colour or bleached, it can be easily dyed at home. However pre-laundering is recommended to remove the dressing, which resists the dye. Launder prior to sewing as shrinkage may occur.

CANVAS is a heavyweight, plain, tightly woven cotton suitable for upholstery, cushions, blinds and outdoor furniture. Often referred to as sailcloth, duck or drill, it is available in a wide range of colours or may be dyed.

CASHMERE is a soft, warm, lightweight luxury fibre which comes from the undersides of certain breeds of goats. Pure cashmere is very expensive as the fibre is scarce. Blends with wool or silk are common, and a more affordable option. Generally used for blankets, throws, cushions and garments.

CHENILLE is French for caterpillar – which is just what soft, cuddly chenille looks like. This fluffy fabric is soft and silky and may be cotton, synthetic or a blend. Popular with lovers of vintage style, traditional chenille bedspreads and bathrobes in good condition are highly sought after.

CHINTZ is made from cotton which has been glazed to produce a patterned sheen. Commonly used for curtains and upholstery as well as table linen. Once very popular for furnishings.

CORDUROY is a reasonably heavyweight, winter style of fabric with a ribbed pattern in the pile. Suitable for blankets, cushions, curtaining and upholstery where a velvety, textured effect is wanted.

COTTON is a natural fibre, commonly used for bed sheets, towels, kitchen linens and curtaining. Quality and width varies, but always look for a long staple fibre and a high thread count.

DAMASK is a durable, reversible fabric often made from cotton, silk or wool. Used for bed and table linen, it has subtle stripes or patterns. Damask has a distinctive, lustrous sheen which not only looks good but also helps to resist soiling. Popular in white, damask is also available in a wide range of colours.

DENIM is made from pure cotton and is commonly used in the garment industry on account of its durability and relaxed style. Denim fabric can be purchased in assorted colours, weights and widths, and is ideal for use as upholstery, curtaining, cushions and quilts.

DRILL is a heavyweight cotton fabric, suitable for upholstery, cushions, heavy curtains and drop cloths.

EGYPTIAN COTTON is an amazingly durable, lustrous and soft fibre which is well known to be one of the best qualities of sheeting available. Suitable for bed and table linens, Egyptian cotton is also made into quality, absorbent towels.

FELT can be either pure wool or synthetic. It is commonly used in craft applications and for wardrobe accessories like bags and hats. Pure wool or felt blends are wonderful for blanketing, cushions and rugs. Hand-dyed, felted items are often considered prized works of art.

FLANNELETTE is a loosely woven, heavy yet soft cotton, wool or blend. Its fuzzy finish is great for winter bed sheets and pyjamas. It varies in weight and texture and is a warm, cosy choice. Especially good for children's sheets and those who like softer bedding.

FLEECE is a synthetic fabric, woven and brushed to create insulating air pockets for warmth. It is not waterproof but can still be reasonably warm even if it gets wet so it's good for outdoor blankets and children's throws.

GINGHAM cotton has a checked pattern and is traditionally used in country designs. Also made into picnic cloths.

HEMP is a natural cloth similar in appearance and performance to linen. It is becoming widely available for furnishings.

HESSIAN is a natural, coarse-fibred fabric often used for covering pin boards.

JACQUARD is named after the French inventor of the loom which produces this highly patterned fabric. The pattern consists of shiny and flat areas, which can be simple in design or highly decorative. Often used for bed and table linens, blankets, upholstery fabric and curtaining. Jacquard is available in cotton, silk, wool, linen and polyester as well as blends.

JERSEY is a t-shirting fabric which is soft and warm, just like the t-shirts you wear. Knitted jersey is not as long-lasting as conventional sheeting – more a fashion item than a classic essential.

LEATHER is made from tanned animal hide. Quality varies according to its suppleness, colour, markings and other individual characteristics. Premium leather (often called 'full top grain') makes a wonderful covering for sofas and chairs. Regular nourishing and buffing will ensure leather remains in good condition.

LINEN is a natural fibre derived from the flax plant. Available in various grades, it is useful as absorbent towelling, table linens, bed sheets, curtaining and upholstery. Use heavier, more durable weights for upholstery and curtaining to ensure the fabric maintains its shape. Linen becomes softer with use and washing.

LOOP cotton makes naturally absorbent bathroom towels and comes in a range of surface textures, including loop, cut loop and velvet.

- **MATELASSE** made from cotton or silk has a distinct, raised, quilted pattern. It is used for bedspreads and cushioning.

- **MOHAIR** is woven from the hair of the Angora goat. Lightweight and warm, it is good for blankets and super-warm, lightweight throws.

- **MUSLIN** is a soft, open weave cotton which is good for sheer curtaining, baby cloths and straining cloths in the kitchen. Available natural, bleached or dyed.

- **OIL CLOTH** is an easy-care, vinyl-permeated cotton fabric suitable for tablecloths, aprons and work surfaces which need regular wiping clean with a damp cloth.

- **ORGANDY** is a fine, transparent cotton with a crisp finish suitable for sheer curtaining and cloths.

- **ORGANZA** is a transparent, sheer fabric often used in curtaining. It may be made from polyester or silk.

- **PERCALE** is a term used for cotton sheeting with a lightweight yet strong, soft weave. Percale bed sheets can either be 100% cotton or a blend, usually 50/50 cotton/polyester.

- **PIMA COTTON** is an excellent quality, durable, soft fabric suitable for bed sheets and table linen.

- **POLISHED COTTON** is either a satin or plain weave cotton that has been machined to produce a shiny appearance.

- **POPLIN** is a wrinkle-resistant cotton/polyester blend commonly used in the garment industry but also suitable for easy-care sheeting. Once very popular but less widely available these days.

- **RAYON** is a reasonably soft, durable, moth-resistant fabric made from cellulose fibres and commonly used in upholstery, curtaining, carpets, table linens and bedspreads. As it's prone to shrinkage, dry cleaning is recommended. Rayon can also be ironed with ease with the correct heat setting on the iron.

- **SATEEN** is made by weaving strong, long-fibred cotton to produce a shiny surface on the fabric. Commonly used in making lustrous, durable bed sheets.

- **SATIN** is a silky fabric which may be natural or polyester. It is often used in sheeting, lingerie and pyjamas. Also used as a trim for curtaining, cushions, blankets and sheets.

- **SEERSUCKER** is a lightweight cotton fabric with a puckered surface texture. Used mostly for tablecloths – vintage styles in good condition are popular.

- **SILK** is a natural, luxury fabric made from the cocoons of silk worms. Incredibly strong and lustrous, it can be easily dyed and is warm in winter and cool in summer. Available in various blends and weaves, it is commonly used for bed sheeting, cushioning, lamp shades and throws. Launder silk with care.

- **SILK SHANTUNG** is a sumptuous silk that comes from the Chinese province of Shantung.

- **STRETCH LEATHER** or leatherette is a synthetic fabric designed to look like real leather. It is used for upholstery, cushions and furnishings.

- **SUEDE CLOTH** can be made from wool, cotton, rayon, synthetic or blends. It mimics the look and feel of real suede leather, has a soft nap and is excellent for durable, easy-care, clean-lined upholstery and cushions.

- **SUEDE LEATHER** is made from animal (usually kid) skin. It has a softly textured and supple finish, suitable for binding and covering furniture, boxes and accessories, general upholstery and cushioning.

- **TAFFETA** is a lustrous fabric, made from silk, rayon or synthetic fibres. Crisp and rustling, it has the tendency to crease easily. Used for silky cushions, bolsters and to make stunning curtaining.

- **TERRY TOWELLING** is a looped pile, absorbent cotton fabric that is either woven or knitted. Used mostly for towels.

- **THAI SILK** is used for curtaining, bed linens, cushions and table runners and is lightweight with a beautiful shimmer.

- **TICKING** is tightly woven, durable cotton often used on mattresses, quilts or pillows to stop feathers poking through. Traditionally plain white or striped in black or blue, ticking may also be used for general upholstery, curtains, accessories and lampshades.

- **VELOUR** is French for velvet and has a pile or napped surface which looks like velvet. Cotton velour is the most common type used for home furnishings; it is suitable for cushions, curtains, bedspreads, general upholstery and accessories.

- **VELVET** is a plush fabric with a low pile on one side which looks and feels soft. Available in a range of qualities, weights and fibres including silk, rayon, cotton, wool or synthetics. Higher quality velvet is more durable and crushes less. Commonly used for specialist upholstery, curtaining, general upholstery, trims, accessories and scatter cushions.

- **VELVETEEN** is made from cotton or cotton-blended fabric to produce a short, dense pile similar in look and feel to velvet, but more durable. Commonly used for cushions, curtains, bedspreads and general upholstery.

- **VINYL** is a durable, easy-care fabric with a polyester backing, available in various grades and colours. Suitable for indoor upholstery, cushioning and table coverings. Marine grades will withstand weather and can be used for outdoor furniture.

- **VOILE** is a beautiful, sheer, loosely woven fabric which hangs and gathers well. It can be made from plain cotton, wool or a polyester blend and is most suitable for crisp, sheer curtaining.

- **WOOL** is renowned for its softness and warmth and is used for bed quilts, under-blankets, throws and pillows. Lambswool and merino are among the softest wools available. Camel, goat and alpaca are also popular for home furnishings. Quality varies: price is usually a good indicator.

STONE & TILES

- **BRICKS** new or old, can be used to pave floors. They have a beautiful, rich, red/brown, rustic appeal. If laid and sealed well, bricks create a highly practical, durable surface; they can be arranged in various patterns. Suitable for both indoor and outdoor use, this somewhat unconventional flooring is gaining popularity for its natural charm.

- **CERAMIC TILES** generally have either a glazed or unglazed surface.
  - Glazed ceramic tiles are popular for their durability and ease of care. The tile has been fired to produce a hard, non-porous surface that is easy to wipe clean.
  - Unglazed ceramic tiles are generally slip resistant and show little wear, making them excellent underfoot in high traffic and commercial floors as well as in laundry and utility rooms.

- **COMPOSITE STONE** looks like the real thing but has been made from natural stone which is crushed, cleaned and re-formed with resins. There is a wide range of colours and styles to choose from. A popular choice for wall, floor and bench surfaces in kitchens and bathrooms as the surface colour and finish is non-porous; however sealing is often required for stain protection and added durability.

- **ENCAUSTIC TILES** have their colours and patterns literally fired into the body of the tiles. They can be laid on floors both inside and out, without risk of the pattern loss usually associated with decorated tiles. Commonly used in Victorian houses.

- **GRANITE** is a hard, hygienic, naturally occurring stone commonly used for kitchen and bathroom areas because of its ease of care with no sealing required. Its high durability and resistance to scratching and staining makes it ideal for high traffic floor and bench areas.

- **LIMESTONE** is a soft, pale-coloured, sedimentary stone. Once sealed, it is both practical and durable and can easily be maintained. Ideal for benches, table tops, floors and walls in either a honed or polished finish. Edges can be square or tumbled to provide a softer effect.

- **MARBLE** occurs when extreme heat and pressure has been applied to limestone. It has a structure which allows it to be honed and polished to a high gloss; this creates the illusion of depth. Its look and degree of patterning can vary enormously, depending on its source. Marble can stain easily but if a penetrating sealer is applied, it can be used for floors, table tops, benches and walls. Clean marble only with neutral products.

- **POLISHED CONCRETE** is a beautiful if less conventional alternative to traditional stone. It can be coloured to suit a wide range of interior styles. The surface is trowelled, honed and polished to produce a finish that is hygienic, durable and easy-care. Suitable for high traffic floors as well as bench tops.

- **PORCELAIN TILES** have been fired at very high temperatures to produce tiles that are dense, non-porous and smooth. Available in a wide range of colours, sizes, thicknesses and surface finishes, porcelain tiles are suitable for walls and floors.

- **QUARRY TILES** have been fired to produce a flat, uniform and fairly industrial looking tile. Available in earthy reds, charcoal, ivory, black and grey.

- **SLATE** is a smooth, soft, natural stone available in a wide variety of textures, colours and sizes. Sealed, it is ideal for wall and floor use, inside and out. As with any stone product, its natural appearance mellows and improves with age.

- **TERRACOTTA** meaning 'baked earth', creates a warm-looking, orange/red flooring for inside or out. Machine-made tiles are more consistent than hand-made tiles in terms of thickness and appearance but have less character. Available either pre-finished or requiring a sealer.

- **TERRAZZO** is made by a process whereby chips of coloured glass, marble, other stones and sometimes fragments of sea shells are mixed in with a cement or epoxy resin base for floor and bench applications. Terrazzo may be laid directly or as tiles. It can be honed or polished to reveal the beautiful chips.

- **TRAVERTINE** is a lovely, soft-coloured stone characterised by its delicate lace and mineral-patterned surface. The naturally occurring voids can be left as is or filled with an ivory coloured resin, then honed or polished. If sealed, travertine is suitable for use on benches, table tops, floors and walls.

- **VITRIFIED TILES** have been fired at very high temperatures to increase their hardness. Generally more abrasion-resistant and uniform in composition than ceramic tiles, they are ideal for walls and flooring and generally require no sealing.

TIMBER & SHEET FLOORING

- **ASH** is a light-coloured, elegant timber varying from creamy white, through to soft yellow and pale brown. Ash has good strength and is used to make furniture and in flooring.

- **BALTIC PINE** is a creamy white to yellow-coloured dense timber with tight knots popular for furniture as well as flooring.

- **BAMBOO** has a light yellow to dark tan colour and a distinctive pattern. Considered environmentally friendly, bamboo is a renewable resource and can be made into high quality furniture as well as laminated flooring.

- **BEECH** is a hard, durable, light cream through to yellow brown timber with a fine grain. Because of its ability to wear well, it is used for furniture and flooring.

- **BLACKBUTT** is an Australian coastal hardwood which is reasonably light to honey brown in colour, highly suitable for flooring.

- **BLEACHING** is a method used to lighten the look of floor boards. The process can be done with commercial wood bleach, a wood wash solution or with lime wax.

- **BRUSHBOX** is a rich looking, elegant timber with a reasonably even grain. Its general colour can vary from pinkish grey to reddish brown, making it a very useful floor timber which can be complementary to a wide range of decorative schemes.

CHERRY is a rich, reddish brown timber with fine graining, popular in the United States for furniture and cabinet making as well as for flooring.

CHESTNUT is a traditional, warm-coloured timber. It is popular as an affordable flooring alternative to oak in many areas of France.

CORK comes from the bark of particular types of oak trees. Cork flooring is porous so it can be painted or stained for decorative effects prior to sealing. Once very popular, especially in kitchen and dining rooms on account of its 'soft fall', but less commonly used these days.

CYPRESS PINE is a pale to golden, brown-coloured timber with distinctive, tight, dark brown knots. Often used as a general flooring timber, it can be stained or lime-washed to produce a variety of shades; however this makes the knotting more pronounced.

DANISH OIL is a traditional timber finish used to protect and enhance timber furniture and flooring. Follow the manufacturer's directions carefully as regards initial and subsequent applications.

ELM has a distinctive grain and a light to mid toning which varies from creamy white through to mid brown. Popular as a reclaimed timber, elm provides beautiful flooring with plenty of character.

FLOATING FLOOR is a term used to describe planks of flooring which are either glued or clipped to each other, and not to the existing floor. Generally they require a cushioned or sound proofing underlay and may be laid quickly and easily over a variety of floorings including concrete and timber. Quality varies considerably, as does price. Sometimes the price quoted by suppliers and tradespeople includes the installation.

FLOODED GUM otherwise known as rose gum, is an Australian coastal timber with an attractive pinkish to brown colouring and straight grain. Commonly used as a veneer for furniture as well as in household flooring.

GRADED TIMBERS are sorted according to quality and price. The appearance determines the grade, not necessarily the strength. Timber choice is ultimately determined by budget and overall appearance required.
• First grade timber generally has the most consistent look and colour.
• Second grade timber may have more inconsistencies.
• Third grade timber is rustic looking, showing the most variance.

HOOP PINE is suitable for flooring and has a smooth finish and warm tone. Once sealed, hoop pine provides a durable floor similar in looks to Baltic pine.

IRONBARK is an extremely hard timber, ideal for structural framing, marine use, poles, decking and floors. Grey or red ironbark makes beautiful strong flooring with rich, warm tones.

JARRAH is a rich, uniform timber with pink to dark burgundy red colouring. The grain is distinct and dark brown to black streaking is also common. Jarrah provides an elegant, deeply toned timber floor which coordinates with a variety of decorating styles and is particularly resistant to insect attack.

KARRI has a pink through to rich red-brown colouring and excellent strength and durability, making it ideal for mid toned flooring.

KILN DRIED simply means the timber has been artificially dried to a desired moisture content for stabilisation, ready for use.

LAMINATED FLOORING is a method of sandwiching together various layers to create a plank. It can consist of a top 'wear' layer, a middle colour, an image or veneer layer, plus a base.

LINOLEUM is a fairly old-fashioned form of sheet flooring often used in schools and hospitals for its hygiene and durability. Naturally made from linseed oil or resin mixed with wood filler or cork stuck to a hessian backing, lino is versatile and gaining new popularity with those seeking environmentally friendly materials.

MAPLE is one of the lightest coloured timber floorings with a white to creamy yellow toning with excellent durability. Once very much in vogue.

OAK has a distinctive grain and is a classic choice for light to mid-toned timber flooring. Known for its performance and durability, the white oak species is popular for 'mission style' furniture with its characteristic graining. The red oak species is popular for flooring.

PARQUET is a term used to describe a classic and beautifully detailed, patterned method of timber floor laying. Made up of many small blocks of hardwood laid in a variety patterns, great skill is generally required to set out, cut and lay this style of flooring. A great choice for new floors, it is often hidden in older style homes in perfect condition, protected by layers of old carpet.

POLYURETHANE finishes may be applied to timber floors to help protect against general wear. Various types, grades and surface sheens are available, depending on the type of application and finish required.

RECLAIMED TIMBER has beautiful character and a multitude of imaginative uses. Source it from salvage yards or check the 'building materials' advertisements in the newspaper.

SPOTTED GUM is an Australian hardwood with a characteristic grain and excellent durability for flooring. Colouring ranges from soft golden yellow through to greyed reds and light browns which when mixed, creates a beautiful 'random' effect.

SYDNEY BLUE GUM is a dense Australian hardwood with deep pink red through to tan and purple brown colouring. Blue gum is a beautifully rich and warm-looking choice for flooring with excellent durability.

TALLOWOOD is a close grained, hard and durable timber which varies in colour from pale yellow shades through to grey and olive grey green. Suitable as a beautiful light to mid tone flooring, other uses include decking and construction.

TASMANIAN OAK has beautiful yellow to pinkish red and mid brown tonings. It makes a very good choice for a light to medium coloured flooring which has excellent durability.

TUNG OIL is a traditional finish for timber floors, providing a mellow, natural-looking sheen with moderate protection.

VINYL is a synthetic form of flooring which comes in sheet or tile form and is extremely practical throughout the home in all rooms, including wet areas. Available in a wide range of colours and designs, vinyl can even look just like natural timber and stone as well as metallic and pearlescent finishes.

NOTE : Information regarding timbers is intended as a general reference guide only and supply may be limited due to availability and country of origin.

CARPETS & RUGS

ABACA comes from woven husks and fibres of Manila hemp and produces a natural, softly textured fibre commonly used for specialised paper products. It was once used in the marine industry, particularly for ropes, on account of its lightness, strength and wear resistance to salt water. Considered softer than coir and sisal, its beautiful texture, lustre and durability makes it ideally suited as a natural floor covering and matting.

BERBER is term used to describe a carpet with random flecks created by the mix of colours in the wool or fibre. Its name comes from the style and colouring of the cloaks worn by the Berber tribes of North Africa. The pile may be cut, twisted or looped in a variety of colours from white and cream through to neutral and brown shades. This type of carpeting is popular for its ability to hide dirt marks.

BRAIDED RUGS are considered the invention of the thrifty. They are made from long lengths of coloured fabric, often recycled, which is braided and stitched together to form round or oval shaped matting. Sometimes they are handed down from generation to generation as family heirlooms.

COIR is made from the hairy fibres of the husk of coconuts. Superior grades can be dyed or woven to produce stunning herringbone and basket-weave styles of natural flooring. Other grades are used for brooms, mattresses and upholstery fill, as well as sacking and matting which is often used for erosion control as well as for the automotive industry.

FLAT WEAVE refers to a technique where no knots are used in the weave. Kelims and dhurries are flat woven and are generally less expensive than knotted rugs as they take less time to produce. Beautiful to have in any home.

HAND-KNOTTED RUGS are considered to be among the best quality rugs. Densely knotted by hand, the value of these exquisite rugs is often determined by the type and number of threads per square inch. The outlay may be largish initially, but in terms of a long-term investment in floor covering it is hard to do better. Always check if professional cleaning is recommended.

HAND-TUFTED RUGS are generally not as expensive as hand-knotted rugs and are made by hand wrapping or using a tufting tool instead of knotting. Threads are secured in place using a backing fabric, usually canvas, which is then glued or stitched to secure.

JUTE is often used for rope, twine and sacking and also produces an incredibly strong, beautiful natural floor covering which looks great in traditional or contemporary settings. Also used as a carpet backing, jute has silky, lustrous fibres and is one of the softest of all natural floor coverings.

LINEAL METRE is how a carpet is sold, rather than by the square metre. A lineal metre is usually 3.66 metres wide and 1 metre long.

NYLON is commonly used in carpet manufacture and is often blended with wool for increased wear resistance and durability. An 80% pure wool and 20% nylon mix is an excellent choice for strength as well as softness.

PILE describes the way the rug or carpet has been threaded. It can be short, long, looped or twisted, each offering a different appearance as well as durability. The density of the pile and type of yarn used will affect how plush or soft the carpet feels underfoot, as well as how well it will wear. Suppliers should be able to give details as to the type of pile and information on the best way to care for the carpet you choose.

POLYESTER is a sturdy synthetic fibre, often blended with wool or cotton in carpets and rugs to increase durability, water-resistance and general washability.

SISAL is derived from leaves of the agave plant. The strong natural fibres are used to make a wide range of natural products including floor coverings. For a softer look and feel, sisal is often mixed with wool and can be dyed or woven into different patterns. Sisal is good for floor surfaces where moderate to high durability is needed, for instance in hallways and dining and living areas. In kitchens and bathrooms, use bound pieces as area mats which will be easy to air and dry.

UNDERLAYS are fitted beneath carpets to not only cushion and prolong their life but also to even out minor irregularities in the flooring and reduce noise. Investing in quality underlay really can make a big difference to the overall feel of carpet. It will cost more initially, but it can make the world of difference in regards to the wearability of your carpeting. Non-slip or regular underlay can also be used to provide extra cushioning and grip for area rugs on hard or slippery flooring. It is best to discuss with the supplier and fitter what sort of underlay is recommended for not only the carpet you choose but the type of your existing flooring.

WOOL is commonly used in both rugs and carpeting for its beautiful softness, strength and durability. Available in a wide range of styles and colours, this lovely natural fibre is considered to have a variety of benefits including dirt, stain and moisture resistance. It is also a favourite choice with allergy sufferers, on account of being non-allergenic.

Thanks to Louise and Jennifer Riley who both spent so many hours helping me to research this book. To Nicci, Amanda, Sonia and Belinda as well as Nadine, Janet, Catherine and the rest of the team at Jamie Durie Publishing. To Sophie for being such a cutie, and to Clem and Bob at Star of the Sea. To Dennis Hagger for your gorgeous style, cake and coffee, also thanks to the following suppliers for research assistance, props and location assistance:

RESEARCH, PROPS AND LOCATION ASSISTANCE :

- Aeria Country Floors (02) 9362 0900 www.aeria.com.au
- Marg Butler of Anasazi Homewares (02) 9698 2225 www.anasazihome.com
- Bed Bath 'N' Table (03) 9387 3322
- Bliss Upholstery (02) 9439 1077
- Boyle Industries (03) 9874 2266 www.boyleindustries.com.au
- Bristol Paints Hornsby (02) 9477 5677
- Coco Republic (02) 9436 0133 www.cocorepublic.com.au
- Dennis Hagger of Cote Maison (02) 9745 5400
- Dupont (02) 9923 6111 www.dupont.com
- Milners Homewares – Le Creuset 1800 099 266
- Noritake Australia (02) 9316 7123 www.noritake.com.au

- Riedel Asia Pacific (02) 9025 3998 www.riedel.com
- Royal Doulton Australia (02) 9499 1900 www.royal-doulton.com
- Sealy Australia (02) 9604 0044 www.sealy.com.au
- Sleepmaker and Dunlopillow www.sleepmaker.com.au
- Villeroy and Boch (02) 9975 3099 www.villeroy-boch.com
- Waterford Wedgwood Australia (02) 9899 2877 www.waterfordwedgewood.com.au

NOTE: Colour swatches shown within the Colour chapter are my own personal mixes which I refer to when buying paint, materials and accessories. You may also find them useful as a colour guide when shopping.

Special thanks to Jamie. Over many wheel barrows and piles of dirt, we have talked for so long about this book and finally, it's here. Thank you for sharing, and producing my vision and for allowing me the freedom to write and create my own story. I am so grateful for your belief, passion, enthusiasm and support.

To Avalon, my beautiful girl, AKA the Book Orphan. Thanks you gorgeous thing, for your love, hugs, ideas and patience, as well as for your fabulous food and endless cups of tea. And to Martyn, not only for capturing such life and spirit throughout this book with your stunning photography but also for your true friendship and love, thank you.

Index

Conversions chart

LENGTH MEASURES

METRIC *millimetres / centimetres*	IMPERIAL *inches / feet*
3mm	⅛ in
6mm	¼ in
1cm	½ in
2cm	¾ in
2.5cm	1 in
5cm	2 in
6cm	2½ in
7.5cm	3 in
10cm	4 in
13cm	5 in
15cm	6 in
18cm	7 in
20cm	8 in
23cm	9 in
25cm	10 in
28cm	11 in
30cm	12 in (1 ft)
60cm	24 in (2 ft)
90cm	36 in (3 ft)
120cm	48 in (4 ft)
150cm	60 in (5 ft)
180cm	72 in (6 ft)
210cm	84 in (7 ft)

LENGTH MEASURES CENTIMETRES (CM);
MILLIMETRES (MM); FEET (FT); INCHES (IN)

LIQUID MEASURES

METRIC *millilitres*	IMPERIAL *fluid ounces*
30ml	1 fl oz
60ml	2 fl oz
100ml	3 fl oz
125ml	4 fl oz
150 ml	5 fl oz (¼ pint/1 gill)
190ml	6 fl oz
200ml	7 fl oz
250ml	8 fl oz
280ml	9 fl oz
300ml	10 fl oz (½ pint)
500ml	16 fl oz
600ml	20 fl oz (1 pint)
1000ml (1 litre)	32 fl oz (1¾ pints)

ONE AUSTRALIAN METRIC TABLESPOON (TBSP) = 20ML
ONE AUSTRALIAN METRIC TEASPOON (TSP) = 5ML
ONE CUP = 250ML (8 FL OZ)

DRY MEASURES

METRIC *grams*	IMPERIAL *ounces / pounds*
15g	½ oz
30g	1 oz
60g	2 oz
90g	3 oz
125g	4 oz / ¼ lb
150g	5 oz
180g	6 oz
200g	7 oz
250g	8 oz / ½ lb
280g	9 oz
300g	10 oz
310g	11 oz
375g	12 oz / ¾ lb
500g	16 oz / 1 lb
1kg	32 oz / 2 lb

OVEN TEMPERATURES

	CELSIUS	FAHRENHEIT	GAS MARK
Very Slow	120	250	½
Slow	150	300	2
Moderately Slow	160	325	3
Moderate	180	350	4
Moderately Hot	190	375	5
Hot	220	425	7
Very hot	245	475	9